CAMBRIDGE
UNIVERSITY PRESS

477 Williamstown Road, Port Melbourne, VIC 3207, Australia

Cambridge University Press is part of the University of Cambridge.

It furthers the University's mission by disseminating knowledge in the pursuit of education, learning and research at the highest international levels of excellence.

www.cambridge.org
Information on this title: www.cambridge.org/9780521711012

© Greg Bowden & Kerryn Maguire 2008

This publication is in copyright. Subject to statutory exception and to the provisions of relevant collective licensing agreements, no reproduction of any part may take place without the written permission of Cambridge University Press.

First published 2001
Second edition 2004
Third Edition 2008
Reprinted 2009, 2012, 2013, 2014

Designed by Marta White
Typeset by Marta White
Edited by Bree DeRoche

A catalogue record for this publication is available from the British Library

National Library of Australia Cataloguing in Publication data
   Bowden, Greg (Gregory Laurence).
   Practice IT. Book 1 for lower secondary.
   3rd ed.
   Includes index.
   For lower secondary students of IT.
   ISBN 9780521711012 (pbk.).
   1. Computer programs - Problems, exercises, etc.
   2. Word processing - Problems, exercises, etc. I.
   Maguire, Kerryn. II. Title
005.36

ISBN 978-0-521-71101-2 Paperback

Reproduction and Communication for educational purposes The Australian Copyright Act 1968 (the Act) allows a maximum of one chapter or 10% of the pages of this publication, whichever is the greater, to be reproduced and/or communicated by any educational institution for its educational purposes provided that the educational institution (or the body that administers it) has given a remuneration notice to Copyright Agency Limited (CAL) under the Act.

For details of the CAL licence for educational institutions contact:

Copyright Agency Limited
Level 15, 233 Castlereagh Street
Sydney NSW 2000
Telephone: (02) 9394 7600
Facsimile: (02) 9394 7601
Email: info@copyright.com.au

Reproduction and Communication for other purposes Except as permitted under the Act (for example a fair dealing for the purposes of study, research, criticism or review) no part of this publication may be reproduced, stored in a retrieval system, communicated or transmitted in any form or by any means without prior written permission. All inquiries should be made to the publisher at the address above.

Cambridge University Press has no responsibility for the persistence or accuracy of URLs for external or third-party internet websites referred to in this publication and does not guarantee that any content on such websites is, or will remain, accurate or appropriate.

The author and publisher wish to thank the following for permission to reproduce material:

© Commonwealth of Australia reproduced by permission, www.australia.gov.au, pp. 37 bottom, 45, 46; Deakin University, p. 37 top; Google screenshots reprinted with permission from Google Inc., pp. 1 left, 3 (google), 29 bottom, 30, 34 top; Istockphoto/ Chris Schmidt, p. 50; Microsoft product screen shots reprinted with permission from Microsoft Corporation, pp. 13, 29 top, 33, 47 left; Northern Territory Government, pp. 31, 32; Photodisc, 10 bottom right; Shutterstock, p. 4 (cube)/ Bartosz Ostrowski, p. 43 bottom right/ BelleMedia, pp. 1 right/ 3 (internet)/ Ilja Masík, pp. 3 (dvd), 177 top/ Poznukhov Yuriy, p. 3 (health)/ 3poD Animation, p. 14 right/ Alan Freed, p. 5 (rocket)/ Albo, pp. 7 left, 10 top centre/ Antonis Papantoniou, cover, p. (i)/ Arman Zhenikeyev, p. 43 top right/ Artmann Witte, p. 7 centre left/ Broeb, pp. 1 bottom, 7 centre right/ David C. Rehner, p. 4 (apple)/ Dino Ablakovic, pp. 14 left, 23 left/ Eimantas Buzas, p. 12 top centre/ Galina Barskaya, p. 43 top left/ IKO, p. 4 (mouse)/ Iofoto, p. 24 top/ Iryna Kurhan, pp. 5 (cd), 177 right/ Juha Sompinmäki, pp. 5 (rings), 12 bottom centre/ Keellla, p. 5 (camera)/ Laurence Gough, p. 43 bottom left/ Lev Olkha, p. 5 (pay tv)/ Lynne Furrer, p. 5 (imac)/ Marcin Balcerzak, p. 24 centre/ Mushakesa, p. 12 top right/ Natalia Bratslavsky, p. 12 bottom left/ Pascale Wowak, p. 3 (education)/ Patricia Malina, p. 3 (games)/ Perrush, pp. 47 top, 49/ Petr Vaclavek, p. 10 top left/ PhotoSky 4t com, p. 43 centre/ Prism 68, p. 12 bottom right/ Ritu Manoj Jethani, p. 4 (moon)/ Robert Elias, p. 25/ S-dmit, p. 14 bottom/ Sebastian Kaulitzki, p. 4 (bomb)/ Slawomir Fajer, p. 11/ Stephen Coburn, pp. 1 centre, 7 right, 23 right, 24 bottom/ TimmyQ, p. 3 (banking)/ Tiplyashin Anatoly, p. 4 (disk)/ Victoria Alexandrova, p. 3 (shop)/ Vivid Pixels, p. 4 (baby)/ Wallenrock, p. 11/ Yuliyan Velchev, p. 10 top right/ Zaichenko Olga, p. 14 top/ Bet Noire, p. 21/ Bruce Rolff, p. 22/ David Davis, p. 75/ Kiselev Andrey Valerevich, p. 38/ Mathieu Viennet, p. 125/ Miodrag Gajic, pp. 109 centre, 171/ Nikolay Titov, pp. 133 centre, 145/ Putchenko Kirill Victorovich, pp. 47 right, 155 right/ Steve Baker, p. 176/ Tebenkova Svetlana, p. 187/ Yuri Arcurs, pp. 18, 79 right/ Duettographics, p. 94; Yahoo! Inc, reproduced with permission of Yahoo! Inc. 2007 by Yahoo! Inc. YAHOO! and the YAHOO! logo are trademarks of Yahoo! Inc., p. 34 bottom.

Every effort has been made to trace and acknowledge copyright but there may be instances where this has not been possible. Cambridge University Press would welcome any information that would redress this situation.

Teachers' notes	v

Module 1 — 1
Computer awareness

Introduction	3
Recent history of computer development	4
How a computer works	6
Computer hardware	6
Network communications	11
Graphical user interface	13
Storage and memory	14
Computer security	17
Computer crime	20
Firewalls	21
Communication – internet and email	23
Internet features and services	27
Using an address to open a website	29
Moving around a website	32
Using search engines	33
Netiquette – internet etiquette	35
Useful information?	36
Bookmarks or Favorites	38
Sending and receiving email	39
Cyber health and safety	42
Internet project	46

Module 2 — 47
Word processing

What is word processing?	49
Keyboard technique	49
Entering a document	50
Formatting text	52
Copying and pasting text	54
Inserting page breaks and moving text	55
Tab stops	57
Page margins and indents	58
Combining tabs and indents	60
Further tabs and indents	61
Bulleted and numbered lists	62
Leader characters	63
Page formats	66
Inserting graphics	67
Multiple page documents	68
Using sections	69
A more detailed newsletter	72
Word processing project	74

Module 3 — 79
Microsoft Office drawing tools

Drawing Shapes	81
Editing objects	82
Enhancing shapes	84
The Text Box tool	86
Using Clip Art	87
Using WordArt	89
WordArt enhancements	90
SmartArt Graphics	91
Aligning objects	92
Drawing tools project	94

Module 4 — 95
Making Movies

Getting started	97
Motion and video effects	99
Making movies project	106

Module 5 — 107
Multimedia

What is multimedia?	109
Creating a new presentation	109
Inserting graphics	112
Starting from scratch	113
Slide transitions	115

Animating slides for a slide show	116	**Module 8**	**177**
Building bullets	117	**Databases**	
Using masters	118	Database terms	179
Movie clips	124	Creating a database	179
Action buttons	125	Editing a database	181
Creating a custom action button	127	Creating reports	181
Multimedia project 1	130	Calculation fields	182
Multimedia project 2	131	Creating different reports	183
		Sorting data	184
		Finding data	185
		Databases project	186
Module 6	**133**		
Computer graphics		Index	188
The different types of graphics programs	135		
Creating a painting	135		
Making a more detailed sketch	137		
Copying graphics	139		
Editing graphics	140		
Introduction to photo editing	141		
Special effects	146		
Combining many photographs into one	147		
Adding text to images	152		
Computer graphics project	153		

Module 7 — 155
Spreadsheets

What is a spreadsheet?	157
Spreadsheet structure	158
Data entry	159
Formulas and calculations	159
Formatting	165
Charts	167
Using Goal Seek	172
Spreadsheet project 1	175
Spreadsheet project 2	176

Teachers' notes

Introduction

Practice IT has been developed to provide practical computing activities for students in years 7 and 8. Students have far greater access to computer equipment in schools now and specific Information Technology subjects are being introduced, or current subjects are introducing computer units – for example, Spreadsheets in Mathematics.

The aim of the book is to cater for both scenarios by breaking the book up into a series of modules. Some modules could be used in current subjects and others in a separate Information Technology subject, or all the modules could form the Information Technology course.

The book also aims to cater for different teaching methods by providing brief instructions followed by an activity.

Software

Guide notes are available for the following software package on CD:

Internet:	Microsoft Internet Explorer, Firefox
Word processing:	Microsoft Word 2007, Microsoft Word 2008
Microsoft drawing tools:	Microsoft Word 2007, Microsoft Word 2008
Making Movies:	Microsoft Moviemaker, iMovie
Multimedia:	Microsoft PowerPoint 2007, Microsoft Powerpoint 2008
Computer graphics:	Photoshop CS, Microsoft Paint
Spreadsheets:	Microsoft Excel 2007, Microsoft Excel 2008
Databases:	Microsoft Access 2007, Filemaker Pro

Other software may become available. Please check the Cambridge website for updates.

Teaching suggestions

The modules can be completed in any order, although it would be advisable to do Module 3 ('Microsoft Office drawing tools') before completing Modules 4, 6 and the second half of Module 2. Module 1 ('Computer awareness') can be completed in stages over the two years. Many of the activities could be set for homework. You may also prefer to do the internet and email sections early in Year 7.

The table opposite provides an example of how the modules could be used over the two junior years.

Year 7	
Module 1	Computer awareness exercises 1–8 About the internet exercises 1–3 Internet exercises 1–9
Module 2	Word processing exercises 1–9
Module 3	Microsoft Office drawing tools exercises 1–12
Module 5	Multimedia exercises 1–9
Module 6	Computer graphics exercises 1–4
Module 7	Spreadsheets exercises 1–15
Year 8	
Module 1	Computer awareness exercises 9–12
Module 2	Word processing exercises 10–16
Module 4	Making movies exercises 1–8
Module 5	Mulitmedia exercises 10–24
Module 6	Computer graphics exercises 5–9
Module 8	Databases exercises 1–8

Sample projects

Sample projects are provided at the end of each module.

Extension activities

Students who complete all the activities can be extended using *Practice IT Book 2 (Third Edition)*.

Sample graphics and data sets

Sample graphics and data sets for use in the modules 'Word processing' and 'Computer graphics' can be found on the Cambridge University Press website at www.cambridge.edu.au/education/PIT.

MODULE 1

computer awareness

Introduction

There is more to information technology (IT) than playing the latest game on a home computer. IT affects every part of our lives, even if we not are aware of it. We have control over some systems, while others are out of our control (we can only trust that those systems are used appropriately).

IT is used in everyday life – in programmable items such as video and DVD players, air-conditioning systems and public transport ticketing.

IT is used in work – in office administration. IT is used in health care – to record patient care, analyse test results and administer medicine and other procedures.
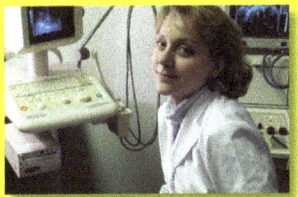

IT is used in communication – to access the internet and to send and receive emails.

IT is used in education – to produce reports and assignments, deliver lessons and for research.

IT is used for shopping – in computerised registers and computerised stock control.

IT is used for banking – to record all banking transactions and bank online, which has revolutionised the way we can do banking.

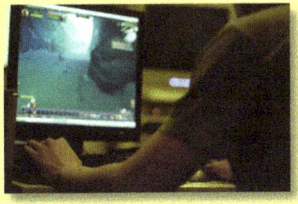
IT is used in entertainment – in computer games, playing and producing music, producing videos, and in animated movies, such as *The Simpsons Movie*.

MODULE 1

Recent history of computer development

The following timeline shows the development of the computer industry in relation to significant events in world history. Read through the timeline and see if you can identify the significant computer-related developments.

Computers		World events	
	1945	Hiroshima bombed 	
ENIAC – first large-scale computer	1946		
'Bell' transistor	1947		
	1949	Adidas trainer released	
First commercially available digital computer	1951		
Commercial production silicon transistors	1954		
Integrated circuits	1958	First skateboard	
Mouse patented 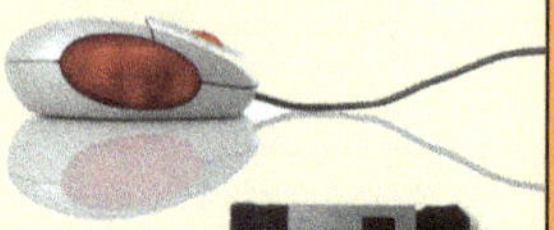	1963	US President John F Kennedy (JFK) assassinated	
Floppy disk 	1967	Australian Prime Minister Harold Holt disappears	
Window, mouse–keyboard idea	1968		
RAM chip	1969	First man walks on the moon 	
	1970	Pocket calculator	
	1972	CAT scanner	
	1974	VCR / Cyclone Tracy (Darwin)	
Microsoft founded	1975	Colour TV in Australia	
Apple computers 	1976		
	1977	Rubik's cube 	
Space Invaders (computer game)	1978	First test-tube baby born 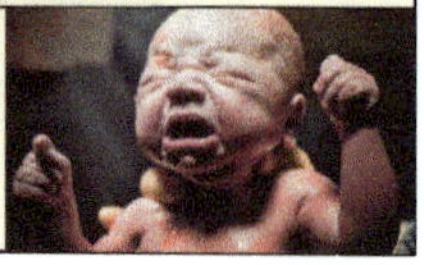	

computer awareness

4

	1979	Post-It notes	
	1980	John Lennon assassinated	
	1981	Prince Charles and Lady Diana married	
Apple Lisa – first graphical user interface / CD-ROM	1983	Ash Wednesday bush fires / *Mash* (TV series) ends	
	1984	Carl Lewis wins four gold medals at the Los Angeles Olympics	
Windows released	1985	Tetris invented	
	1986	Challenger space shuttle catastrophe	
Microsoft releases Works	1987		
Word for Windows	1989	Berlin wall falls	
Work begins on the first feature-length computer-animated film: *Toy Story*	1990		
	1992	*The Cosby Show* (TV series) ends	
First Encarta	1993	Fred Hollows dies	
Digital camera / Zip drive	1994		
Windows 95	1995	*Babe* (film) / Pay TV	
	1997	Princess Diana dies	
Apple iMac / Windows	1998		
Year 2000 bug	1999		
Stephen King e-book	2000	Sydney Olympic Games	
	2001	September 11	
	2002	First Bali bombings	
Apple iPod	2003		
Proliferation of Broadband	2004	Boxing Day Tsunami (Thailand)	
	2005	Second Bali bombings	
YouTube	2006	Beaconsfield mining disaster	
Windows Vista	2007		

How a computer works

No matter what type of computer system you use, they still work the same way:
- input of data
- memory for storage
- central processing of data
- output of data.

The way a computer works can be likened to how you process a task. For example:
1. You receive a homework sheet from your teacher.
2. You store it in your folder until you have time to do it.
3. You work on the homework sheet, producing the answers.
4. You give the completed homework sheet to your teacher.

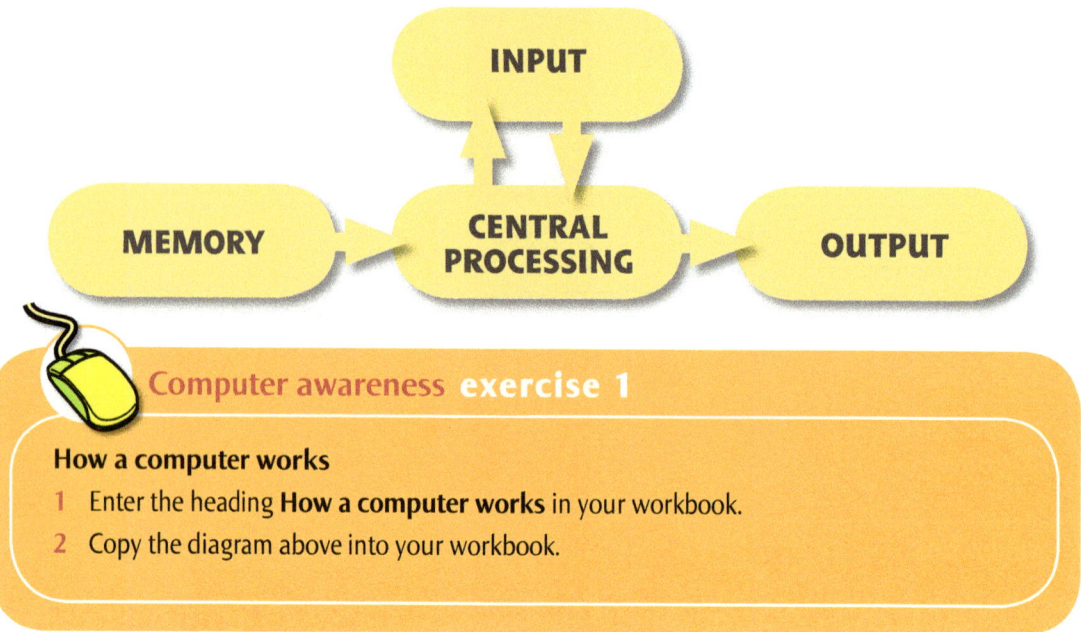

Computer awareness exercise 1

How a computer works
1. Enter the heading **How a computer works** in your workbook.
2. Copy the diagram above into your workbook.

Computer hardware

In general, a computer allows us to:

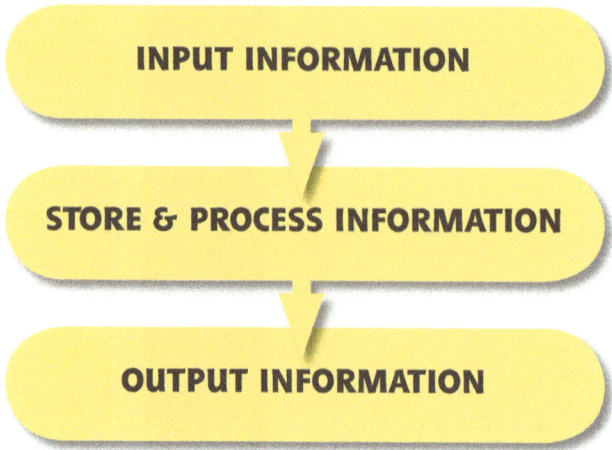

On the opposite page are the typical components of a computer system that enable each of these phases.

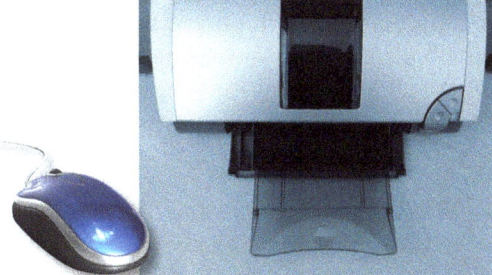

System unit | Keyboard – input | Mouse – input | Printer – output

Monitor – VDU output

The power of computers lies in their ability to store and process data. However, a computer must have a way of getting the data into itself. Devices such as the **keyboard** and **mouse** are used to **input** data.

Computers can also manipulate information, such as presenting it in different ways or performing calculations. A computer can do these things because of **programs** located on the **system unit**. A program is a set of instructions to the computer telling it what to do with the information we give it.

The **information** can be **output** using devices such as the **screen** and the **printer**.

The **input** and **output** devices are often called **peripherals**.

The **mouse** and the **keyboard** are common **input** devices. The **screen** and the **printer** are common **output** devices. However, there are many other devices we can use to get data into the computer and then to get it out. You might recognise some of these devices listed below.

Input devices	Output devices
Keyboard	Screen – visual display unit (VDU)
Mouse	Printer
Scanner	Plotter
Modem	Modem
Digital camera	Digital projector
Recorder	Floppy disk drive
Light pen	Speakers
Magnetic ink character recognition (MICR)	Synthetic speech
Optical mark reader	Flash drive
Joystick	iPod / MP3 player
Touch screen	
Touch pad	

There are many computerised devices that do not look like a traditional computer at all. For example, a video recorder is computerised. The input device to program the video recorder is the touch pad or buttons on the video player – or it may be the remote control, which also has buttons. The output device is the digital display on the player, which shows what is happening – for example, DVD recording.

Computer awareness exercise 2

Input and output devices

1. Copy this table into your workbook. (You will need about 12 rows.)

Input device	Output device

2. Write the names of these hardware devices in the Input device or Output device columns of your table.

digital camera	modem	scanner
iPod	mouse	screen – VDU
joystick	optical mark recorder	touch pad
keyboard	plotter	touch screen
light pen	printer	
MICR	projector	

Computer awareness exercise 3

Peripheral devices

Choose six peripheral devices (three input and three output) and find out some information about them. Write a paragraph about when the device is used and what type of data is entered or output using the device. For example, a visual display unit is used to display the results of using a program, such as a picture you have created in a graphical program.

Computer awareness exercise 4

Computerised devices

Find three examples of computerised devices at home, or at school. Identify the input device used to put information into the computer. What is the job of this device? Identify the output device. What is the job of this device?

Some examples of devices on which you could focus are:

- CD player
- microwave
- supermarket cash register
- mobile phone
- automatic teller machine (ATM).

Computer awareness exercise 5

Computers and places

Think about the places you or your family visits in any two-week period and take note of any computerisation that you observe.

1 List at least two places you have visited.
2 What is the purpose of the computer being used in each place?
3 How big is the computer in physical size (i.e. hand-held, desktop)?
4 How many people can use the computer at once?
5 What other places could use a similar computer?

For example, a library uses a computer to record information about books, record borrowing and borrowers' details. A computer could also be used to produce flyers and other documents such as posters and book reviews.

Other places you may visit that might use computers are:

- school
- supermarket
- doctor's surgery
- sports centre
- large retailer (i.e. Target)
- small retailer (i.e. local store)
- video store
- post office.

The development of technology

As the range of input and output devices increases, the range of tasks a computer can perform improves. This means that many more people can be helped by the use of a computer.

For example, in relatively recent times the main method of getting text into a file was to use the keyboard. Scanners improved this with special software that enabled blocks of text to be scanned into a file. With the development of voice recognition software and appropriate hardware, many people can now enter text and give commands simply by speaking to the program. This is an amazing development for people who have physical difficulties with typing.

Entering pictures into a document was limited to using Clip Art or drawing a picture from scratch. Scanners improved this with the ability to scan a picture into a file, which could then be inserted into a document. Now digital cameras can take pictures directly, then the digital picture file can be inserted straight into the text file.

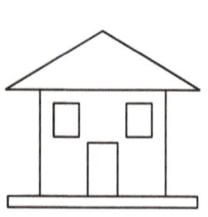  

Computer awareness exercise 6

Voice recognition software

1. Find out how voice recognition software works.
2. What hardware do you need to use voice recognition software?
3. What advantages would this type of software have over typing?
4. What disadvantages are there in using this software?

Computer awareness exercise 7

Digital cameras
1. Find out how a digital camera works.
2. What hardware do you need to use it?
3. What advantages would this type of technology have over Clip Art?
4. What disadvantages are there in using this piece of technology?

Network communications

Communication components such as modems are now part of a standard computer system. Later in the chapter you will learn more about modems. Network connections are other common devices in computers that enable them to be connected to a network, commonly used in schools and offices. Wireless technology also connects computers and is becoming more popular.

A network is created when two or more computers are connected by a modem, network cable or wireless technology. Each point on the network that connects a device is called a node. A network within a small area such as a room, building or buildings close together such as a school or hospital is called a local area network, better known as a LAN.

This diagram illustrates a typical network structure where all the computers can communicate with each other. One computer acts as the host, or server.

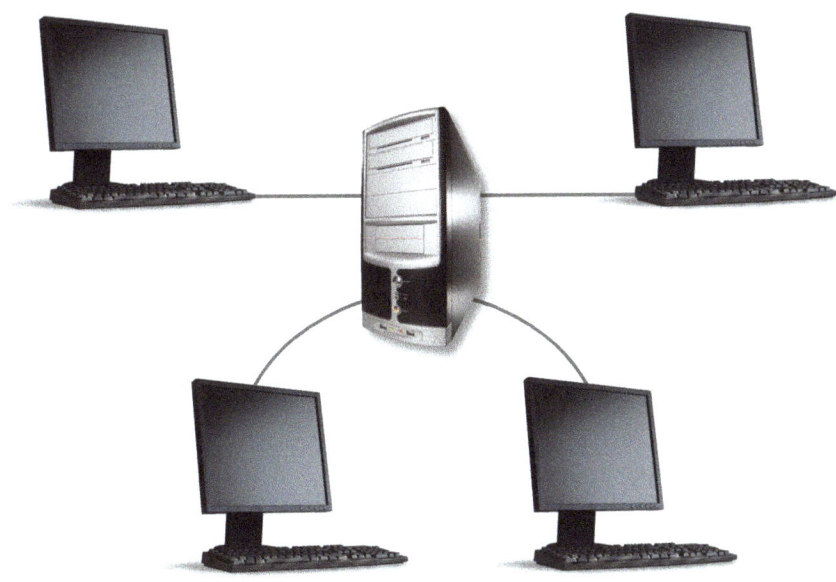

There are many benefits in using a network, the main being the need for fewer peripheral devices. Prior to networking, each computer would probably have a printer connected to it to print documents. In a network, only one printer is required as each computer communicates with the printer via the network. Other advantages lie in the ability to access files and programs on other computers and communicate via internal email.

Computer software

A computer program is a set of instructions that determine the steps that a computer performs when it processes data. There are many different types of computer programs.

Standard, relatively inexpensive programs can be bought from retailers – for example Windows, Microsoft Word, Corel Draw, as well as hundreds of games. Microsoft Word is a word processing program used in millions of businesses, schools and homes around the world to produce documents.

Customised programs can be developed to work in a specific way for a business or organisation. There are many programs developed for businesses that the person on the street would use without realising. For example, an ATM machine uses a customised program to perform financial transactions on a user's bank account. Supermarket cash registers use scanners to input the data into a program that then stores the data or may update an inventory program.

Many household appliances contain computer programs to control the way they work. The Y2K problem (also know as the Year 2000 problem, or millennium bug) in many pieces of equipment highlighted just how many everyday items are affected by computer programs.

Operating systems

A computer's **operating system** is a program – or programs – that control the operations of a computer. The operating system determines how each hardware component of the computer system is used. The operating system enables us to print a document while opening a file or entering text. It also provides an interface (or meeting point) between the user and the programs. The interface – sometimes known as the **graphical user interface** (see opposite page) makes the computer much easier to use.

Windows is the most common operating system for personal computers. Windows NT, UNIX, Macintosh and Linux are all operating systems. Fortunately, the ordinary person does not need to know specifically about these, thanks to interfaces such as Windows.

Windows is a commonly used interface for the DOS operating system because all programs that work in Windows, while having different functions, have the same Windows qualities. Labels such as 'Word for Windows' or 'This program written for Windows' indicate that these programs have the Windows features.

The name Windows is appropriate because the Windows program allows us to look through 'windows' at the work we are doing in various programs. For example, we might have a word processing program such as Microsoft Word and a spreadsheet such as Microsoft Excel running at the same time. We can use Windows to move from one program to the other quickly, or even view both at the same time.

The Microsoft Windows program has made working on computers much easier and more efficient.

Graphical user interface

The name says it all:

- **graphical** indicates the use of pictures (icons) and colours
- **user** means for the user of the computer
- **interface** is the meeting point between the user and the computer language that most of us don't understand – similar to having an interpreter in a foreign country where we don't understand the language.

A graphical user interface provides a user-friendly means of commanding the computer to perform tasks – for example, **Start** a program, **Open** a file and **Print** files.

It also provides a means for consistency across application programs. A program using Windows uses the common features of the Windows graphical user interface. This makes it easier for the user to learn to use other programs written for Windows as well because the methods of using the program are consistent. For example, within Microsoft Word, Excel, Access and PowerPoint and other Windows programs, the icon to open a file is the same.

It also enables programs to look like their purpose. For example, the Calculator program supplied with Microsoft Windows looks like a calculator.

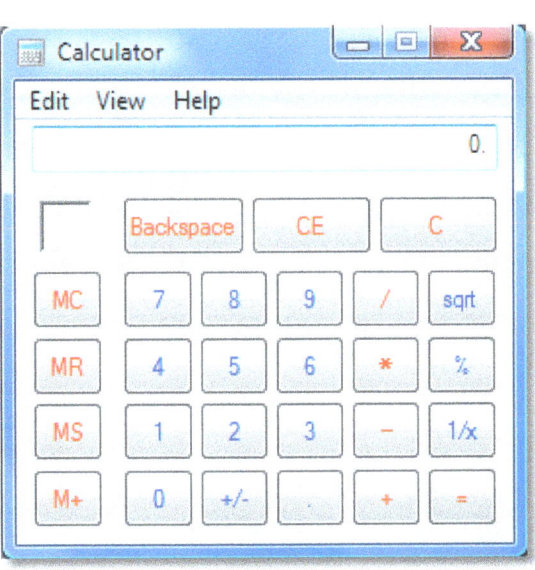

Storage and memory

The power of a computer lies in its ability to store data and programs for use at a later time. This storage can occur in a number of places but it uses essentially the same method.

ROM – read-only memory

This is permanent memory that is used to store very important programs that make the computer work. If anything were to happen to change or delete these programs, the computer would not work. To protect these files they are stored in this special memory called ROM. The files are put into the ROM at the factory when the computer is first made. You cannot access these files. The computer just reads the files each time the computer is started.

RAM – random-access memory

This is a temporary area of memory. It stores short-term data and instructions. Have you ever started a new file, typed in some text, then had the power go off? You turn the computer back on to find that the file is lost. This is because the file is only stored in the RAM – temporary memory – until you actually save it into permanent memory on the hard drive, CD, DVD or flash drive.

When the computer starts up, the RAM is empty until you open programs and start doing things. Then it stores these temporarily until you are finished and close the programs or save the files.

When the computer is turned off, the RAM is cleared out.

The size of the RAM also controls how many programs you can have open at once.

Permanent storage

Every personal computer has a **C:** drive and most have a **D:** drive. The C:\ drive is often known as the **hard disk** or **hard drive**. The C:\ drive is where the computer starts. All programs that a computer can use are stored on this hard drive. When a computer is part of a network, it has access to other drives. Put simply, a **network** is a group of computers connected together so that files can be passed from one computer to another. Printers and other input and output devices can also be connected. Using a network saves time and resources.

Hard drive

Portable storage units are available in the CD and flash drive

Other drive – network

Basic units of stored data – bits, bytes

A drive is a collection of storage bits. One **bit** is the smallest unit a computer can work with – it is the building block of all pieces of data. The term 'bit' is derived from 'binary digit'.

A bit is represented by either a 1 or 0. 1 is *on*, 0 is *off*.

A **byte** is a group of 8 bits. Memory on the computer is divided into bytes. Each character stored uses about one byte of memory. So the word 'elephant' would use about 8 bytes.

1 kilobyte	is	1000 bytes
1 megabyte	is	1000 kilobytes
1 gigabyte	is	1000 megabytes

What are files?

Any work that you create and save with a computer is stored in a file. You provide the **filename** for the work that you create. A file stores information or data. Hundreds of other files exist on the computer that you did not create. These files are installed onto the computer when software is loaded. Each time you install a new game, more files are copied onto the computer.

A computer uses many different files in order to operate. A **program** consists of many different files. Some files make the program run, while others provide the graphics, music and so on. The size of a file depends on how much storage it requires.

What are folders?

Folders are containers for storing files. If your hard disk had only one folder to hold all your files, it would be very difficult for you and your computer to find files, making the task very slow.

It would be a little like having only one cupboard in your house to hold all your stuff. Or think of a library without any shelving. In the same way that having organised storage helps a household to run more efficiently, folders and **subfolders** help a personal computer to operate efficiently.

The files for each individual program are usually kept in their own folder. For example, the Microsoft Windows files are kept in the Windows folder. The Windows folder has a number of subfolders where it keeps files that are related to different tasks within the Windows program.

MODULE 1

Computer awareness exercise 8

Computer terminology

Below is a list of terms that have been covered so far in this book.

1. Create clues for these terms.
2. Use these to construct a crossword in your workbook.

bit	joystick	process
byte	keyboard	programs
digital	memory	RAM
draw	modem	recorder
file	mouse	ROM
floppy disk	network	scanner
folder	output	screen
graphical	peripherals	speakers
input	plotter	user
interface	printer	Windows

3. Make some copies and give them to your friends or other classmates to do to check how good your clues are.

Managing files and folders

We can use **Windows Explorer** or **Macintosh Desktop** (Finder) to manage files and folders. We create files when we save information into the computer's memory so it can be used again.

Windows Explorer provides a picture of how our files are arranged in the computer's memory.

Folders act as the drawers or shelves where the files are stored. They group the files together in a logical manner, which helps the computer (and the user) to locate files easily. As is seen in the opposite diagram, just as we use wardrobes and drawers to keep our clothes tidy and organised in our home, we use folders in our computer to store files.

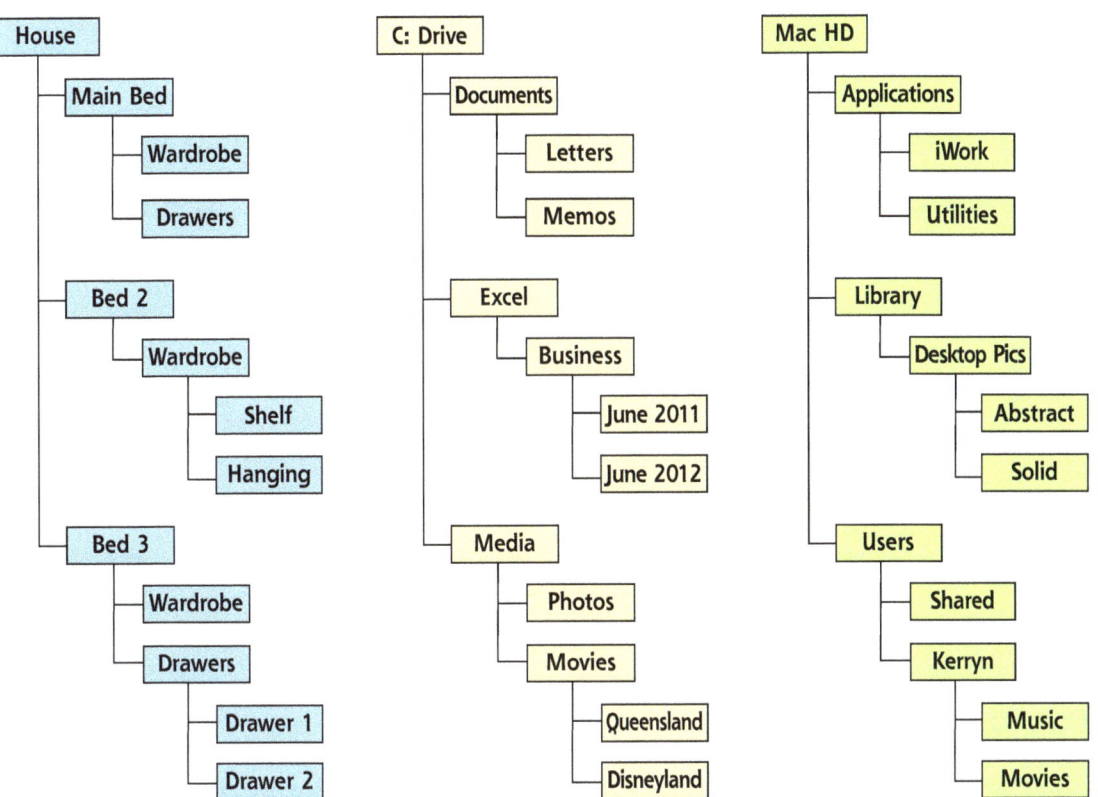

Computer security

We use computers for more than just playing games. We use them to create letters, projects and pictures. Businesses use computers to record sales and purchases, business plans and other information. The information we store on computers is often very important and needs to be protected. We need to protect it from physical damage or theft. We should also protect it from other people trying to use it without our permission. In addition to this, we need to be aware of where we put our information, and from where we get our information.

Backup data

Backing up is an easy way of protecting our data. Backing up is just making a copy of a file and putting it somewhere away from its usual location. Backup files can be stored in a number of different ways.

zip disks	will hold 100 MB
superdisk	will hold 120 MB
CD	will hold 600 MB
flash drive	will hold at least 4GB
portable hard drive	will hold up to 500 GB

Most word processing files and simple desktop publishing files are small, so many can be stored on one CD. Some graphic and video files are too large and need something larger on which to be copied, such as a flash drive or a portable hard drive.

Backups should be performed regularly – you should always think in terms of *when* the files are ruined, rather than *if*, because that will make you remember to backup often. It's better to take the second to do it rather than regret it later when you lose your data because you didn't make a backup. If you are wondering how often you should do backups, just think of how much work you would have to redo if something happened to your files. Some people backup every half an hour or so, while others backup every few minutes. It's up to you. You are responsible for your own files. Do not rely on others to look after them.

Computer awareness exercise 9

Computer security
1 How does your school do backups?
2 What is a good way for you to do backups?

Passwords

Another way you can protect your files is through the use of passwords. Only the person who has access to the password can open particular files or programs. But be careful: setting a password means you have to remember it or have some way of retrieving it.

Computer awareness exercise 10

Passwords
1 How does your school secure its computers?
2 What is a good way for you to protect your files?

Computer viruses

One reason to backup important files is the threat of virus damage to your computer and files. A computer virus is a small program that attaches itself to other programs and hides until it is ready to strike. The 'strike' is often activated by a date. Email viruses often attach themselves to email and multiply in a similar way to a chain letter. Computer viruses are programs written by malicious people, who create them for no other reason than the personal satisfaction of destroying other people's computer systems (and often making news headlines), having no regard for the damage it causes to often thousands of people.

It is very important that you backup important files so that you have a copy of the file to fall back on should a virus cause serious trouble on your computer.

There are some simple steps for protecting yourself from viruses:

- Load antivirus and firewall software onto your computer.
- Try not to use other people's disks – you don't know where they have been or if they have been properly virus protected.
- Always scan emails, disks and programs for viruses.
- Update the antivirus and firewall software regularly.
- Perform regular Windows updates.

Computer awareness exercise 11

Computer viruses

1. Write the heading **Computer viruses** in your workbook.
2. List the steps for protecting your computer from viruses.
3. Why is each step important?

Computer awareness exercise 12

Antivirus software

Look up the following sites on the internet for the software companies listed and find answers to the questions below.

McAfee Viruscan   www.mcafee.com
Vet Premium   www.vet.com.au
Norton AntiVirus   www.symantec.com

1. What is the cost of the antivirus program?
2. Will the program scan email?
3. Does the company give free updates and for how long?

Computer crime

Computer crime is the illegal use of a computer system for personal benefit. Some common criminal acts are:

- stealing data from a company computer system
- deleting data from a company computer system
- altering accounting records.

Many computer crimes are difficult to prove. It is often very difficult to identify who committed the crimes because the person may have used another's password to access the system.

Hackers

'Hacker' is the name given to people who try to access systems by guessing passwords or other measures to access the system. In an effort to combat hacker activity, it is now an offence to gain access to a computer without authority.

Malicious damage

Viruses can cause serious damage to computers. It is often difficult to determine who originally sends or creates the virus. It is also difficult to prosecute the person even if they are found.

Computer theft and fraud

Computer theft covers a wide range of crimes. People might steal data from a computer that does not belong to them. For example, an unhappy or spiteful employee at a large company might steal sensitive financial information and reports from a computer and sell it to a rival company.

Stealing software or computer equipment is also a crime, just as is stealing any item that does not belong to you.

Another way of stealing software is by making copies of it. This is called software piracy. It is illegal to make copies of software and distribute them to your friends or sell them.

Computers as criminal tools

A computer has many uses for criminals today to perform other offences. For example, counterfeiting money is much easier now with the use of a computer. Identification cards and credit cards are also much easier to fake using a computer.

Firewalls

Another way to protect your computer data is to implement a firewall. Firewalls work like a security door, inspecting data as it enters and leaves an organisation's network. Without a firewall, a virus can enter a network before it is detected. If you think of a network as a house with many rooms, each lockable from the inside, a virus that gets in the front door can then attack any room that is left unlocked.

An organisation would never dream of leaving their front door unlocked at night and relying on each employee to lock their respective offices. Yet they may leave their network open to virus attack by not setting a firewall application in place.

A firewall works by checking all emails, files and every piece of data before allowing them into the organisation's network. The pieces of data are compared to a database of known problem data, much the same way as scanning for known viruses. If a match is found, the data is blocked and so prevented from reaching the network.

A firewall can also control the information that can be sent from the computer onto the internet without your knowledge such as personal details, banking details and passwords, etc.

Increasing use of the internet and the sophistication of hacker activity has inspired the increasing use of firewalls for personal computers at home. A computer that is connected to the internet is essentially part of a network and so must be protected, not just from viruses, but from hackers too.

To get the best from a firewall, you should ensure the following:

- Set the firewall to maximum security levels.
- Make regular backups of your important files.
- Update the firewall regularly.
- Only allow internet access to programs you are sure are legitimate.

You can find more information about firewalls at these sites:

McAfee Internet Security	www.mcafee.com
Norton Internet Security	www.symantec.com.au
PC-cillin 2003	www.trendmicro.com.au
Look 'n' Stop	www.soft4ever.com

MODULE 1

Computer awareness exercise 13

Computer crime

1 Look up a recent copy of the IT section of *The Age* or *The Australian*, published on Tuesdays.
2 Scan through the articles to find any on computer crime.
3 Which of the types of crime on page 20 does the crime in the article match?
4 Summarise what the person or group did – or what the crime is and how it affected the victim.
5 How would you feel in the following situations?
   - Someone finds your copy of *Tomb Raider*, which you paid $70 of your hard-earned money for. They make copies of it and give it to all their friends.
   - Someone makes copies of your science project and gives them to the rest of the class.
   - Someone finds an email you sent to a friend that contains stuff you don't want anyone to see. They print out 50 copies and post it around the school for everyone to see.
   - Someone gets your password and sends lots of nasty messages from your email account (pretending to be you) to your friends.

Communication – internet and email

The internet has opened the world to an explosion of possible communication between tens of millions of people across all continents. Businesses can use the internet to advertise and publish information, buy and sell goods and services, and access information from competitors' prices to travel timetables, to the latest business news to government documents.

They can send and receive electronic mail from colleagues and clients, link computer networks across national and international borders, transfer files from one location to another, and conduct banking services such as transferring funds, paying bills and checking account balances.

Internal and external networks

Networks are created when computers are connected to each other in order to communicate, share resources and transfer information. In your school, if your computer is linked to other computers in the same area, the network is known as a local area network (LAN). If your computer is linked to a school in Melbourne or Sydney or Bendigo, then the network is probably a wide area network (WAN). The internet is a worldwide collection of many thousands of computer networks. It is, in fact, a network of networks that can relay information within seconds to almost anywhere around the world.

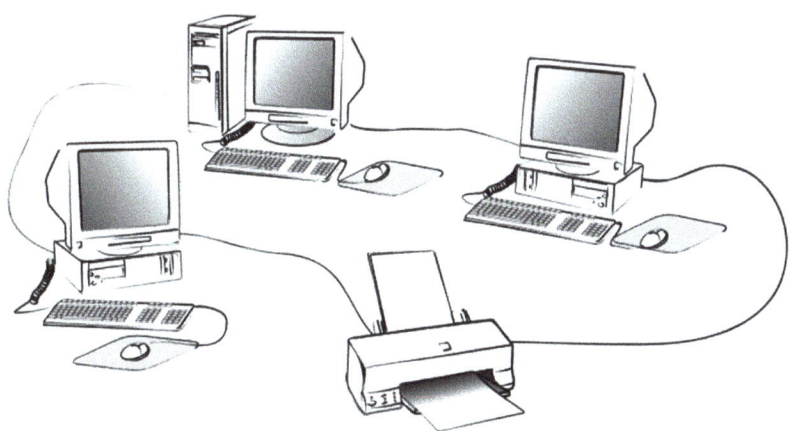

The development of the internet

The internet began in the United States in the early 1960s. The Department of Defense's Advanced Research Association (ARPA) developed a small network to allow the sharing of information between military personnel and scientific researchers. This was called the **ARPANET**. ARPANET was enhanced to withstand a military attack from an enemy by maintaining communication even if one or more of the computers became unavailable. The system was based on a standard set of rules, called **protocols**, that defined how computers would communicate, much the same as people have implicit rules for speaking to one another. The ARPANET grew to include universities throughout the USA and a few overseas. The military became concerned that the increased use of the network could endanger national security and decided to sever its links with the ARPANET. This paved the way for academics to expand their use and for business interests to initiate commercial use of what has become the internet.

Today, no organisation or body owns the internet but it is regulated and controlled by some responsible authority in each country, normally a communications company. Until 1995 Australia's part of the internet was regulated by the Australian Academics Research Network (AARNET), which was funded by universities and other academic institutions. These days Telstra is responsible for maintaining the required infrastructure and coordinating all access to the internet across Australia.

Who uses the internet?

Scientific researchers and university academics

We know that scientific researchers and university academics were active in the early beginnings of the internet, and their involvement continues today. They use the internet for distributing, searching and retrieving files and articles, corresponding via email and providing educational sites involving audio, visual and interactive capabilities.

Business organisations

Business organisations use internal email extensively on their LANs and WANs but also access the internet to communicate nationwide or worldwide. They promote business ideas and concepts, advertise and trade goods and services as well as keeping an eye on the competition.

Governments

Governments distribute documents such as recent policy development, legislation and parliamentary transcripts. Government departments, at all levels from local to national, use email extensively and provide information on current issues for public benefit.

Online education

Online education is a growing area, touching students from primary to tertiary levels. Students in school on one side of the world can chat with students in another part of the world, get help for their next assignment from an electronic library or access a virtual expert on a range of subjects from maths to medicine. Universities use the internet to distribute educational material and course information, conduct tests and publish end-of-semester results.

Online and interactive learning enables people living in remote locations to have the same educational opportunities as people elsewhere.

Individuals

The internet does not restrict anyone from using its facilities, and people without a computer at home can log on from libraries and schools or work at cybercafes. People can play interactive games, read online books, go shopping, pay bills, look at the stockmarket fluctuations, check out the sports results, read today's newspaper, or browse from site to site – otherwise known as 'surfing the net'.

The future – where do we go now?

Just think of our daily activities compared to those of your parents when they were young – no ATMs, faxes, email, or mobile phones. So where are we heading?
In the future the house may have complete home communication systems, much like cable TV and the internet combined, that will have access to interactive TV, a database of video recordings, educational institutions, cyber shopping malls, online banking and other information services linked by a fast, high-capacity, reliable and affordable communication line. This future scenario is all part of the information superhighway predicted to change the way we live.

Advantages and disadvantages of the internet

There are many advantages and disadvantages of using the net. Can you add to the list that follows?

Advantages

- It provides people with membership to a worldwide library and resource centre.
- It allows greater communication between all people throughout the world and breaks down geographical and cultural boundaries.
- It is changing the workplace environment by allowing people to work from home and remote locations.
- It provides education, health and commercial services to people anywhere in the world.
- It allows people who are otherwise isolated from society for whatever reason to interact with society.
- It provides entertainment and information for millions of people.

Disadvantages

- It can isolate people from direct social interaction.
- It promotes the spread of computer viruses.
- No controlling body verifies the validity of information or restricts illicit material.
- Because knowledge is power, it extends the division between the privileged and underprivileged.
- It enables opportunities for fraud.
- The security of information belonging to individuals, businesses or governments may be jeopardised.

About the internet exercise 1

1. List five advantages of using the internet.
2. List five disadvantages of using the internet.

Hardware and software requirements

A newer computer provides greater speed and memory than an older computer for accessing the internet. This will make the experience more fun as it can be quite frustrating waiting a long time for information to download. That's why some people call the internet the 'world wide wait'. However, if you have a computer that's more than a few years old, don't throw it out just yet. It will still do the job and may suit your needs.

The basic requirements for access to the internet are:

- a computer
- a modem
- a telephone line connection or broadband connection
- communication software
- an account with an internet service provider (ISP).

A **modem** is a piece of hardware that converts digital signals from the computer to analogue signals that can be transmitted across the telephone line (known as **mo**dulation) and converts the analogue signals received from the telephone line back to digital signals for the computer to use (known as **dem**odulation). Recently, the technology has developed and these signals can also be converted via wireless broadband towers, similar to mobile phones. Most new computers have an internal modem. External modems are also available for older computers.

There are currently three types of internet connection: **dial-up**; **cable broadband**; and **wireless broadband**. Dial-up connections require the full use of a **telephone line** and operate fairly slowly. Cable broadband also requires the use of a telephone line, yet operates at double the speed and doesn't disrupt the telephone line, which means you can be on the internet and on the phone at the same time. Wireless broadband, a new technology, is transmitted via **broadband towers** to **PC cards** in computers and is super fast and portable, which means it can be accessed anywhere you can get a signal, both at home and away from home. It won't be long until line-connection is a thing of the past and everyone can connect to the internet anywhere, at any time.

The **communication software** required for connection to the internet is provided free by the ISP on a CD. The installation process sets up the configuration details that the computer needs for connection to that particular ISP.

You will also need to open an **internet account** with an ISP. An ISP (internet service provider) is an organisation or individual that provides a permanent connection to the internet through a host computer and then sells access to the public. With a dial-up internet connection, every time you connect to the internet you have to pay for the telephone call to the ISP's host computer, so make sure that you use an ISP that requires a local call, not an STD call. With cable broadband and wireless broadband, however, it doesn't matter where your ISP is located, so long as you can get coverage in your area. Most ISPs also provide extensive technical support.

Internet features and services

The main internet services available to users are:

- the world wide web (www)
- electronic mail – better known as email
- mailing lists
- usernet use
- internet relay chart (IRC)
- file transfer protocol (FTP)
- electronic commerce (e-commerce).

The world wide web

The world wide web is, as the name suggests, a web of information stored as documents and files of various types located on websites throughout the internet. The web requires a software application called a **browser**, such as Netscape Navigator or Internet Explorer, to connect to the web. This allows websites to be accessed and information downloaded to your computer. Every page of information on the web has a unique address known as a universal resource locator (URL).

A URL for Microsoft is http://www.microsoft.com. The http indicates that the site you want to access uses hypertext transfer protocol (HTTP). This is a type of communication protocol the browser uses to access websites.

Email

Email is extensively used and is a great innovation for anyone with access to a computer. It allows short notes and letters, as well as large documents and files, to be electronically transmitted anywhere in the world within a matter of minutes. Email addresses comprise a user ID, an @ symbol and a domain name. The **user ID** is the user's identification. The **@** symbol is pronounced 'at' and the **domain name** identifies the ISP host computer among all the computers on the internet. The 'com' means 'commercial' (domain) and 'au', of course, means it's an Australian address. For example: userid@domain.com.au.

Mailing lists

Mailing lists are an extension of email. An originator (list owner) advertises for people to share information and opinions on a particular topic and provides an email address to contact if they are interested in subscribing. The originator compiles the list of participants' email addresses and sets up the mailing list. When information is posted to the mailing list email address, all subscribers receive the information.

Bulletin boards

Usenet operates as a collection of bulletin boards or noticeboards known as newsgroups. Unlike mailing lists, no one person is responsible for developing or maintaining these groups but anyone can start a newsgroup. Each newsgroup covers one particular topic and can be used by any number of people by emailing to the newsgroup and sharing opinions on the topic and replying to other messages. Application software such as Internet News is required to access these newsgroups.

Internet relay chat

Internet relay chat (IRC) is the party line of the internet, enabling many people to chat electronically at one time. Messages sent by participants are displayed on the screen, allowing all other participants to reply. There is a certain etiquette to these chat groups and participants are expected to use the greetings 'hello' and 'goodbye' appropriately.

About the internet exercise 2

Imagine that your family has a computer but does not have access to the internet.
1. Write a list of the items you would need in order to get connected to the internet, leaving a few lines between each.
2. Write next to each item the purpose it serves.

About the internet exercise 3

Write a paragraph explaining how each of the following internet services work.
- electronic mail (email)
- chat rooms
- bulletin boards
- websites.

Using an address to open a website

The **address box** is used to enter the address (URL) of the website you want to view. It also displays the address of the website currently displayed on the screen. If you have the specific address of a website you can go directly to it.

- Start your internet browser.
- Click on the address box.
- Delete any text that appears there.
- Type **www.google.com.au** then press the Enter key.

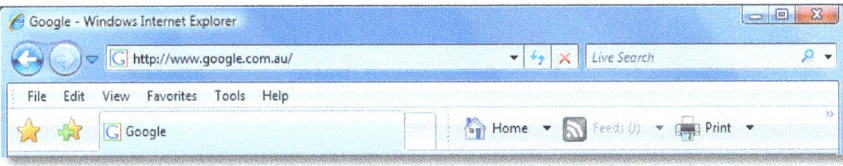

The website for Google will open. Yours may be different from the one shown below.

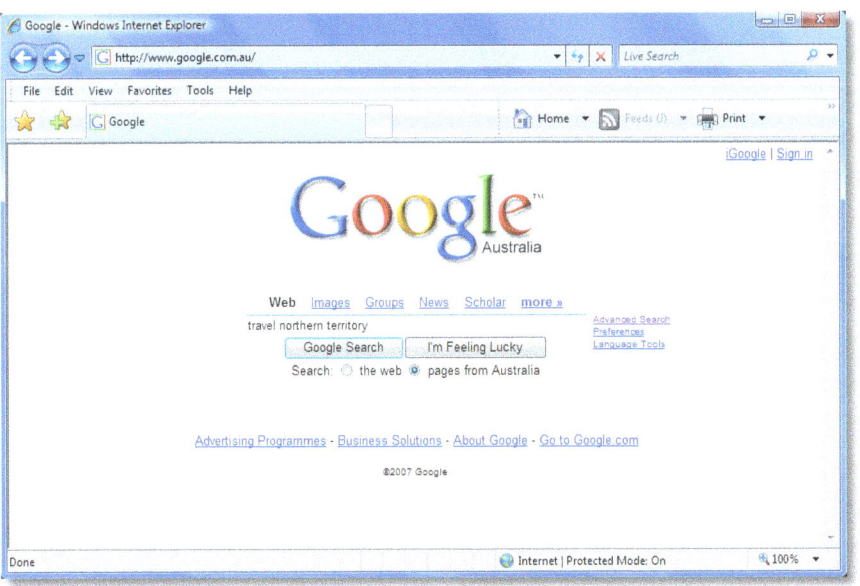

Google is what's known as a **search engine**. It is useful to find sites based on a subject. Suppose you want to look for some information to do with travelling:

- Type **travel Northern Territory** in the white box.
- Click on the Google **Search** button

  Google will search all the websites all around the world in an attempt to find any that focus on 'travel' and 'Northern Territory'. Because it is a rather broad term, the resulting number of sites will probably be large. In this instance, more than **two million** sites were found (which changes daily).

- Click on one of the pages listed.

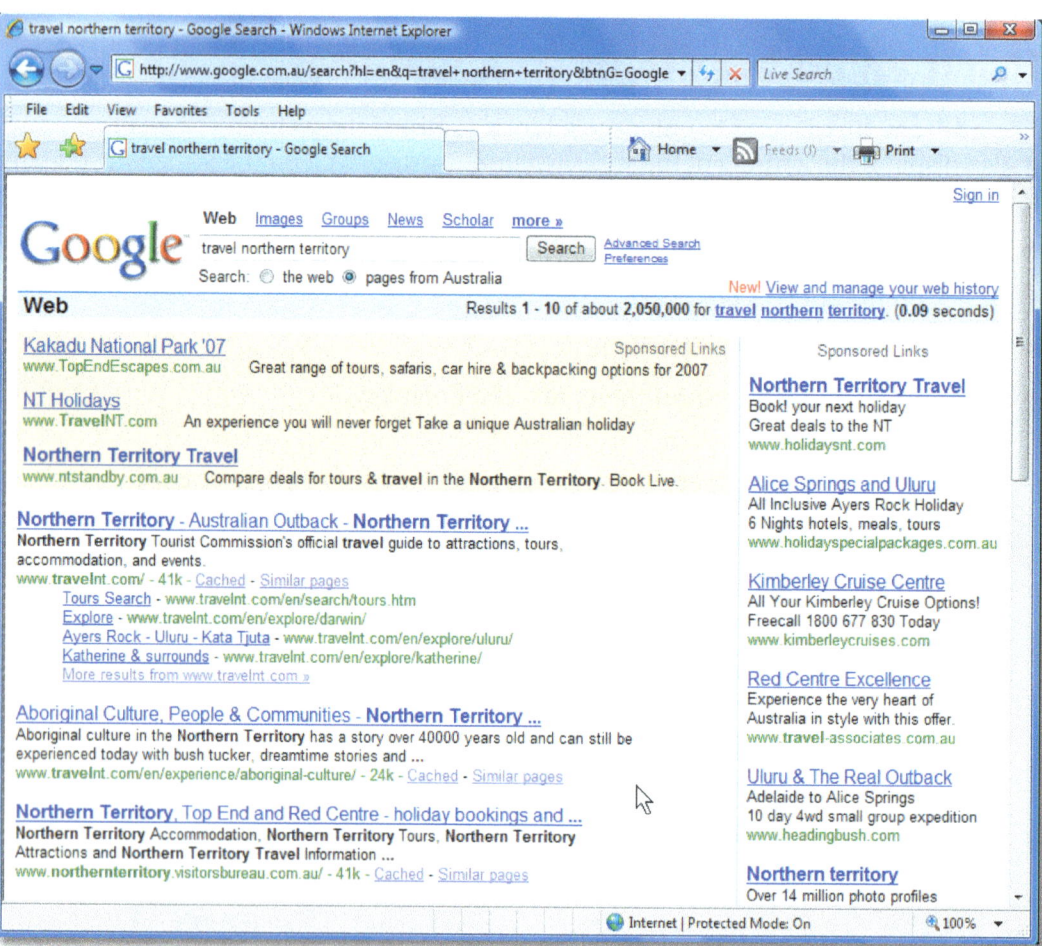

The webpage will open in your browser. From here you can click on links to areas of interest.

- Click on one of the links on the page.

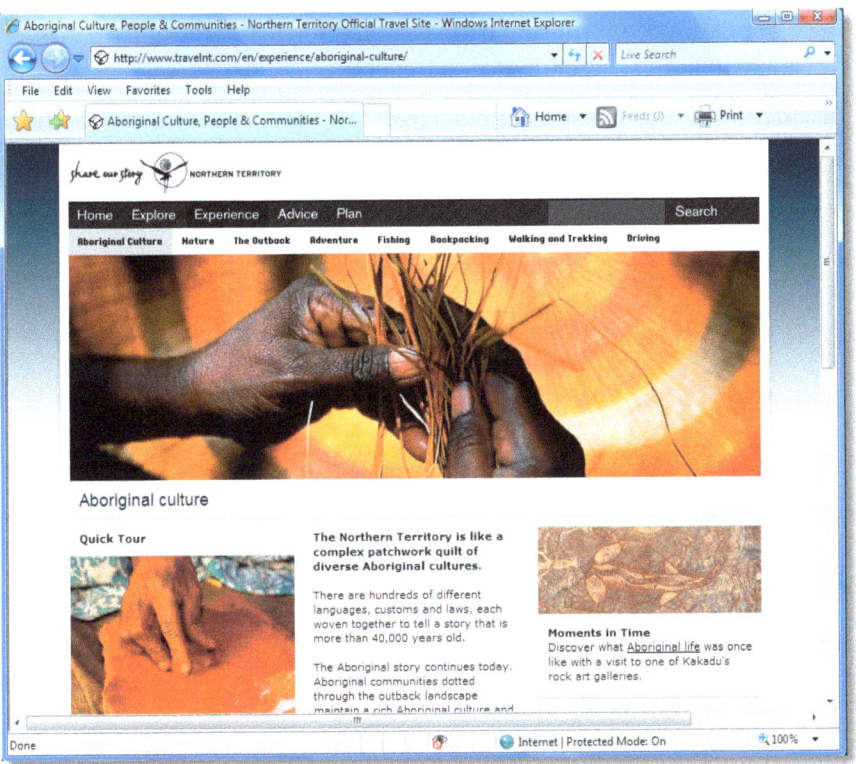

The next webpage will appear.

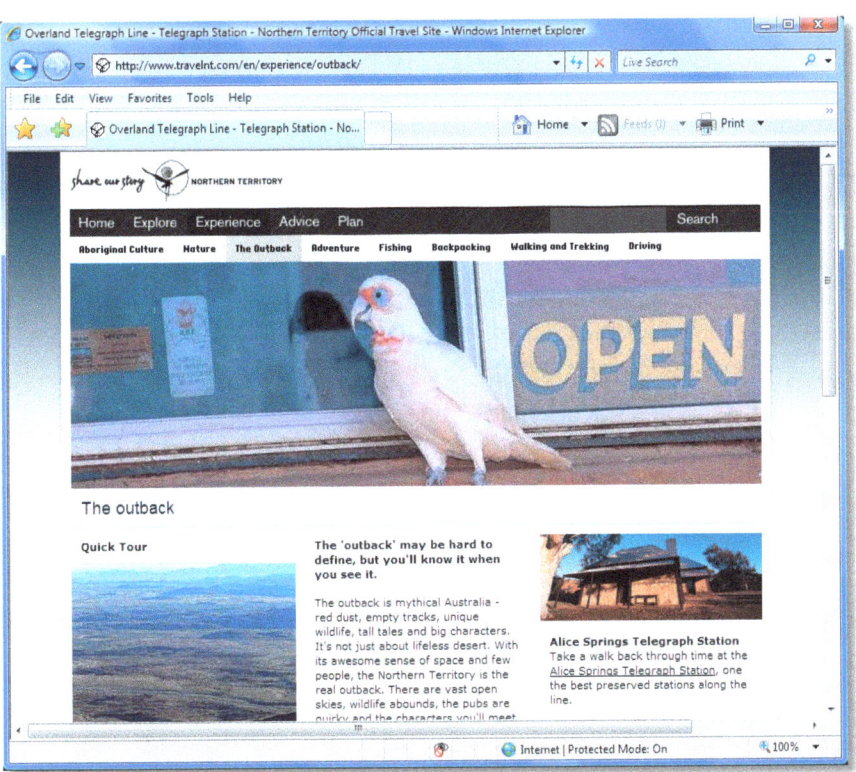

Moving around a website

A website is usually made up of several pages linked with **hyperlinks**. When you click on a hyperlink, Internet Explorer will display the webpage that is linked to that hyperlink. Hyperlinks are indicated in two ways. Any text that is underlined is usually a hyperlink. Some hyperlinks also appear in the form of buttons or pictures. The mouse icon also changes from an arrow to a hand when it is over a hyperlink.

- Move the mouse over the page until it changes to a hand and click the mouse button.

The page to which the hyperlink is linked will appear.

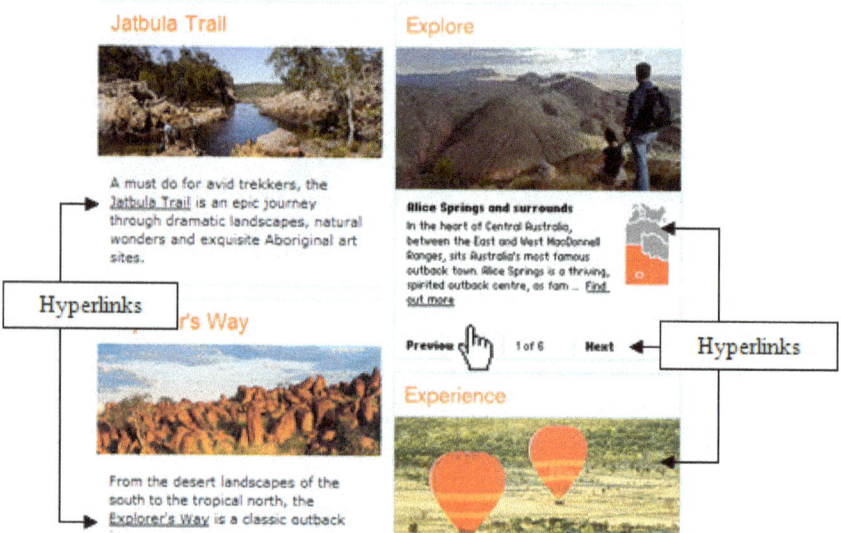

It is quite common that a page will be longer or wider than the screen.

- Use the scroll bar to move down the page.

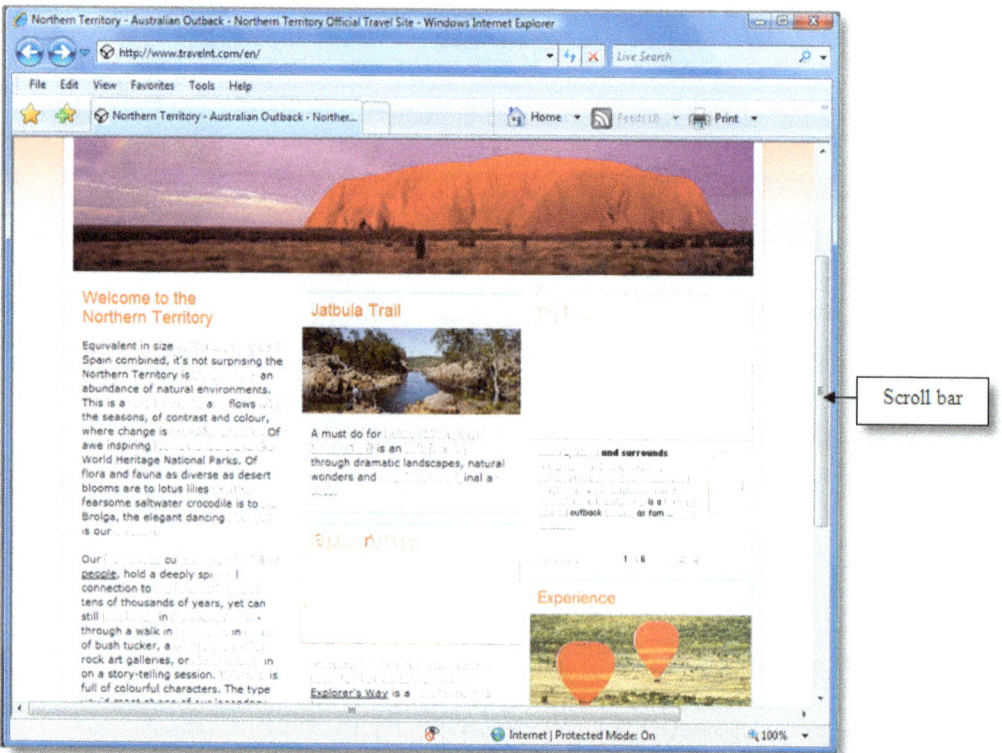

You can make further moves around the site by clicking on other hyperlinks. This is known as 'surfing the net'.

You can move backwards and forwards through the pages you have already visited at any time by clicking on the **Back** button or the **Forward** button in the web toolbar.

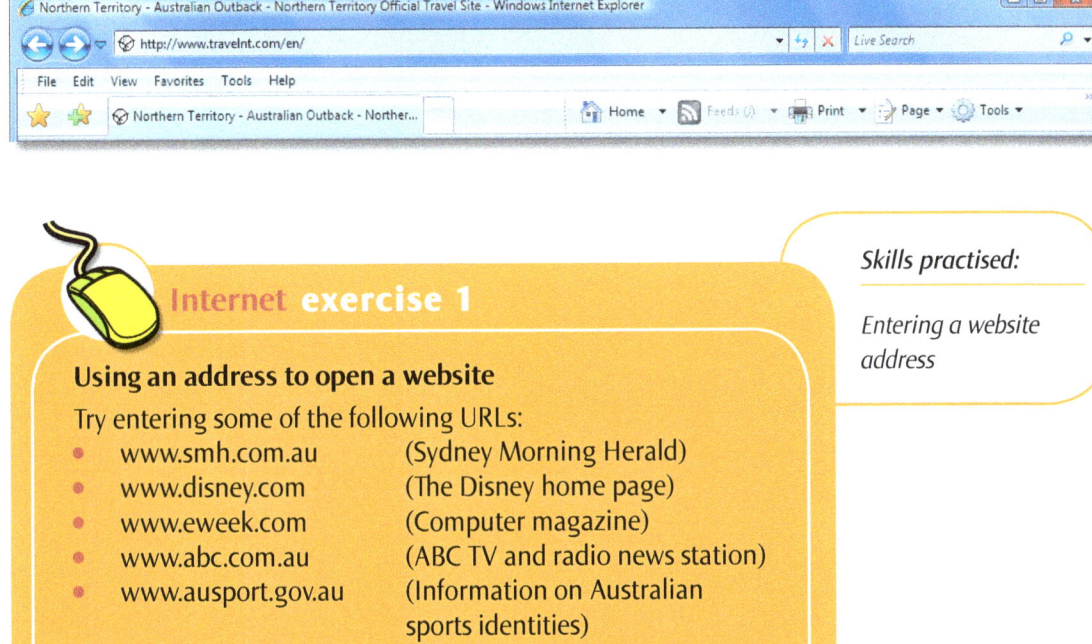

Internet exercise 1

Using an address to open a website

Try entering some of the following URLs:
- www.smh.com.au   (Sydney Morning Herald)
- www.disney.com   (The Disney home page)
- www.eweek.com   (Computer magazine)
- www.abc.com.au   (ABC TV and radio news station)
- www.ausport.gov.au   (Information on Australian sports identities)
- www.ninemsn.com.au   (the Channel 9 news homepage)

Skills practised:

Entering a website address

Using search engines

A search can be more efficient with more words. For example, **accommodation** will produce more sites that are irrelevant than using the phrase **accommodation in Melbourne**.

Another factor that will affect the results is the variance between the search engines. You can type the same phrase in each search engine and they will come up with different results.

- Click on the **Back** button until the first **Google** search page is displayed again, or click on the **address** box, type **www.google.com.au** then press the **Enter** key.
- Type **accommodation in Kakadu** in the **Search** box.
- Click on **Search**.

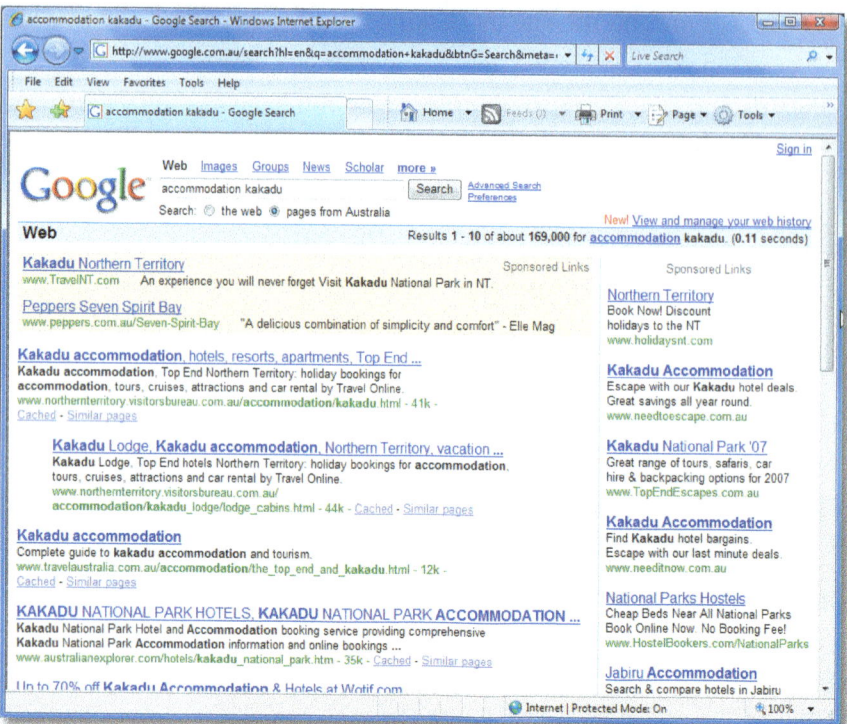

A list of sites will be displayed.

- Click on one of the sites to display it.
- Use the Back button to get back to the Google search page. Google is just one search engine.

Searching the internet

You can use a search engine to conduct a search at any time.

- Type **www.yahoo.com.au** in the web address box.

The **Yahoo! 7** search engine will appear.

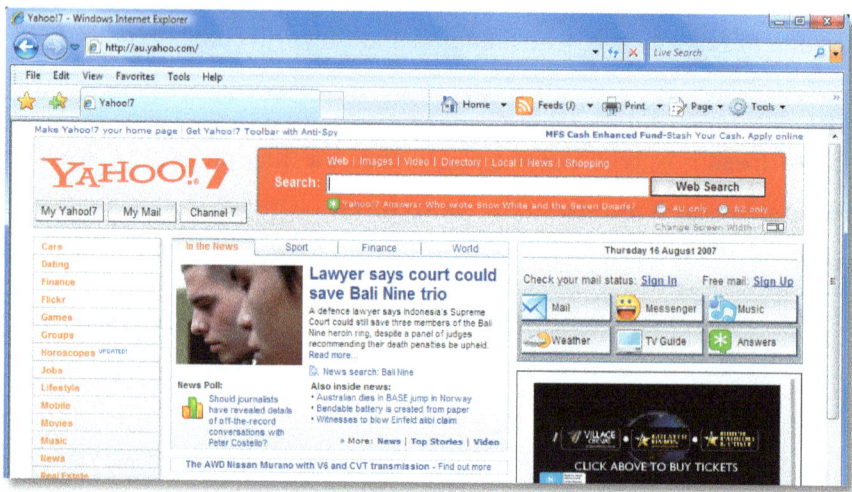

You may have already used the Yahoo! search engine. Some popular web search engines are:

Search engine	URL
Google	www.google.com.au
Infoseek	www.infoseek.com
The Internet Sleuth	www.isleuth.com
Excite	www.excite.com
Live Search	www.live.com

These search engines have different ways of searching and they will produce different results for the same term that is entered in the search box.

Internet exercise 2

Using search engines
Use each search engine listed above to locate an identical term, then compare the results.

Skills practised:

Using a search engine

Netiquette – internet etiquette

'Netiquette' is a new term, meaning etiquette on the internet. Netiquette focuses on how people should behave when using the various services on the internet. For example, YOU SHOULD NOT USE UPPERCASE WHEN TYPING MESSAGES – THIS IS KNOWN AS 'SHOUTING' AND IS VERY ANNOYING TO READ, as though you are indeed shouting.

When using a chat room you could be talking to anyone in any country. It is inevitable at some stage that you will not agree with some of the ideas or statements presented, as people all around the world have different beliefs, religions and points of view. Therefore, you should always be sensitive to the practices, beliefs and opinions of others when chatting with other people on the internet.

There are many excellent sites that provide detailed guidelines on how to behave when communicating with others on the internet.

1 Type **www.yahoo.com.au** in the Address box.
2 Type **netiquette** in the Search box and press Enter.

You should get a decent list of sites.

3 Click in the Address box and type **www.google.com.au** then type **netiquette** in the Search box and click on Google Search.
4 You should get a very decent list of pages. Click on the links to some of the sites to read up on appropriate netiquette.

Internet exercise 3

Netiquette

In this exercise you will create a short report on the results of your searches about netiquette. You may need to repeat the searches.

1. Start a new document in Microsoft Word or a similar word processor.
2. Enter a title for your report and save it with the name **Netiquette Search Report**.
3. Write a brief introduction that states what netiquette is.
4. Name two Search Engines you could use to search for sites about netiquette.
5. Conduct a search using each search engine. List the top five sites displayed for <u>each</u> search in your report. How many sites did your search find in one of the searches?
6. After looking at each of the sites, create your own list of rules – you should be able to list at least eight rules, some for emails and some for newsgroups – some may overlap.
7. Find out the guidelines set down at your school for communicating on the internet and compare them to your own list. Are there any other rules you would add to your own list? If there are, add them to your list.
8. Enter your name and the date at the end of the report
9. Run a spell check, save and close your document.
10. If required, print your report out and submit it to your teacher for checking.

Useful information?

Not everything you read in newspapers and magazines is true. The same applies to the internet. Anyone can put anything on the internet, but publishing it does not automatically make it true. The likelihood of the information being true depends on the author, the date and whether the information is fact or opinion.

Who is the author – are they credible?

Suppose you are looking up information on how to care for a dog and find two sites you think look useful – one by a dog lover, the other by a veterinarian who specialises in pet care. Both sites may have useful information, however, the information provided by the veterinarian is more likely to be factual (i.e. based on study and research), while the information provided by the dog lover is more likely to be anecdotal (i.e. based on personal experience). Even in newspapers, many of the columns are based on opinions, not fact. Simply because someone displays their opinion on an issue does not necessarily mean that it is true or correct. You must consider the author's reputation and qualifications in presenting the information.

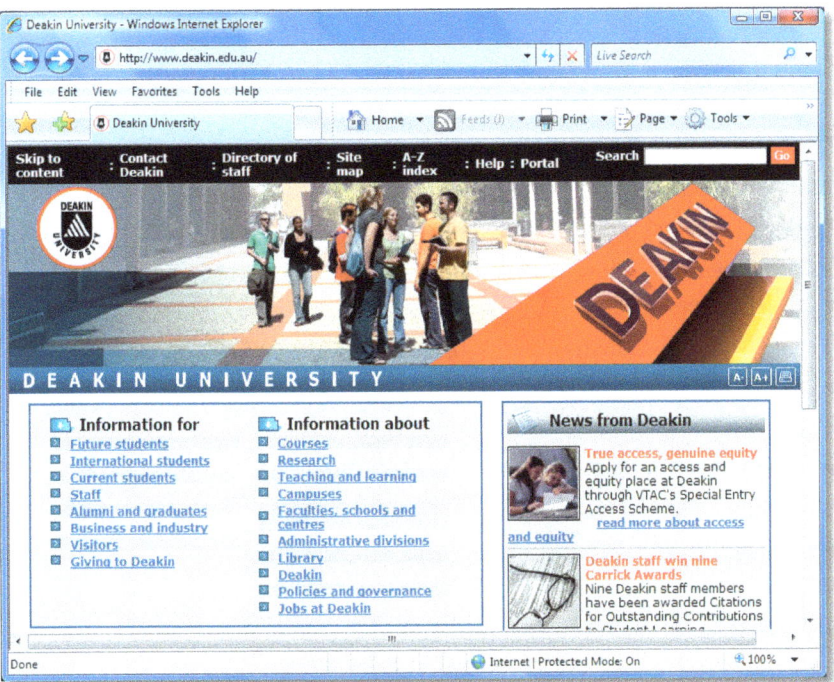

When was it written?

What is the date of information or when was the page last updated? If you are looking for information on the weather, would a page that was last updated two days ago be more or less reliable than a page updated half an hour ago? Would information available on cancer treatment that was last updated a month ago be more reliable than a page that was last updated five years ago? Sometimes, however, the date is irrelevant, as the facts will not change, such as with historical data.

Internet exercise 4

Skills practised:

Entering a website address

Using a search engine

Efficient search methods

Using an internet site

Advanced search

1 Find the Ford Australia site.
  a Find the name, addresses and phone numbers of the Ford dealers in your city or the closest city to you.
  b In the Vehicle Showroom section, find out how many passenger cars are sold by Ford.
2 Find the Harvey Norman site.
  a Name eight product types that Harvey Norman sells.
  b Find four good reasons to shop at Harvey Norman.
3 What does the term 'El Nino' mean? What problem does it cause?
4 Try searching for the Levi Strauss jeans company. In the General Info/Fact Sheet section, answer the following:
  a When were Levis jeans first manufactured?
  b How many million miles of thread is used in the making of jeans each year?

Bookmarks or Favorites

A very useful way of retaining up-to-date information is to store a reference to a site in **Favorites** (Internet Explorer) or **Bookmarks** (Netscape). Then when you want to view the page again you just open the site from Favorites or Bookmarks. This is great for sites you happen to stumble across and want to refer back to. When you want to visit them again you can simply use the reference listed in Favorites or Bookmarks rather that hunting around for it again.

Internet exercise 5

Skills practised:

Using a search engine

Using Favorites or Bookmarks

Add a webpage to Favorites or Bookmarks

1. Do a search for something you are interested in.
2. Display a page from the search results. You have found a page that will be useful. So you can have quick access to the page again, you will now save it in Favorites or Bookmarks.
3. Click on the Favorites or Bookmarks menu then the Add command. The name of the site is automatically entered in the Name box. At this point you can name the reference with a more meaningful name if appropriate (i.e. you might bookmark the Village Cinemas website, yet label it 'movie times').
4. Close the Favorites or Bookmarks window.

Internet exercise 6

Looking up a site in Favorites or Bookmarks

Next time you want to access the site from internet exercise 5, just use Favorites (Internet Explorer) or Bookmarks (Netscape).

1. Click on Favorites in the web toolbar.
2. Click on the site reference you require.

Sending and receiving email

Put simply, email is the sending of messages around a network. The network may consist of a small network of several computers in an office, or the huge worldwide network that is the internet.

A sender sends a message to the central storage area called the **server**. The message remains there until the person it is sent to opens their email and pulls down the message. There are many programs that make sending and receiving email very easy.

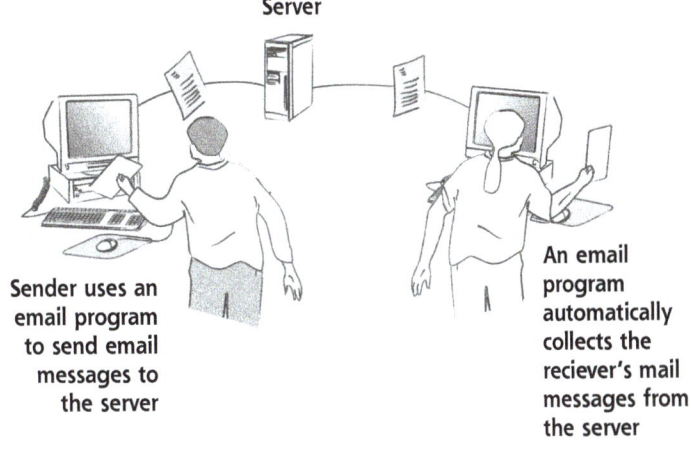

Sender uses an email program to send email messages to the server

An email program automatically collects the reciever's mail messages from the server

Creating a new message

The main components of an email message are:
- The address – who is it to?
- The subject – what is it about?
- The message text.

The address

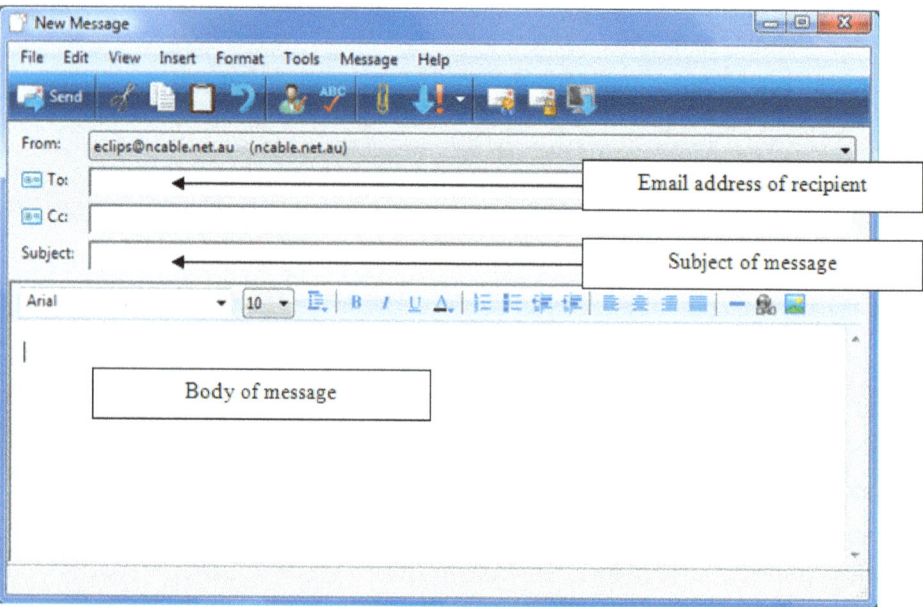

Actual email addresses are needed for people outside your organisation or school network. Mail must be addressed to the person who is to receive it. An accurate address is a necessity for each person who is to receive the message. An example of an email address is **billbrown@bigpond.com**.

The subject

The subject is placed in the subject field at the top of the email, like a heading, and should let the receiver know what the message is about (e.g. Subject: Birthday invitation!).

The message

This is where the actual message is entered. You can generally enter as much text as you need to here (as well as attachments, explained on page 42).

Message etiquette

While emails are a form of letter writing, business email messages are not usually as formal as an actual letter. Even so, confidentiality and privacy rules should apply to email.

- Always read the message before sending to check for spelling and grammar errors.
- Do not use all CAPITALS when typing – it is difficult to read (referred to as SHOUTING, as mentioned previously).
- Keep the message brief.
- Avoid long paragraphs – use white space (line breaks) to make the message easier to read.
- Make the most of the subject line – it will encourage the recipient to open and read the message and also make it easier to find again.
- Limit topics to one subject per email.
- Do not SPAM – that is, mass emailing for the purpose of advertising or chain letters.

Internet exercise 7

Create a new message

1. Create a new message to the classmate on your right.
2. Type their email address in the **To:** box.
3. Type the subject text **Hello** in the **Subject:** box.
4. Type a short message that says hello, and also asks them to reply to you.
5. Send the message.
6. Repeat steps 1 to 5 to send a similar message to the classmate on your left.

Skills practised:

Creating and sending an email message

Using an internet site

Replying to a message

Messages you receive are listed in your inbox. Replying to a person who sent you an email is very easy. Instead of creating a new message from scratch, simply open or highlight the message in the list of messages in your inbox then click on the **Reply** button.

A new message will be created with any extra text to be added.

Attachments

 Files can be attached to email messages very easily. A paperclip icon is commonly used in most email programs.

All you have to do to send an attachement is to create a message as usual with the address, subject and message, then click on the **Attach** button. A window will open, similar to the normal Open file window. Select the file that is to be attached (such as 'English assignment.doc' or 'Birthday invitation.jpeg') and click on it.

When the recipient receives the message, they can open the attached file or save it. But remember: the person you send the file to must also have they same software in which the file was created (such as, for example, Microsoft Word or Photoshop) in order to open it.

Cyber health and safety

 Internet **exercise 8**

Attachments

1. Select two files for sending to others in your class. Select files that you would like some comment on – for example, an assignment or some other file you have created such as a graphic.
2. Create a message and attach the file to the message. In the message ask the recipient to reply to you.
3. Proofread the message then send it.
4. When you receive the reply, make any suggested changes then forward the message to your teacher.

Skills practised:

Creating and sending an email message

Attaching files

Using the internet and mobile phones can be lots of fun. You can chat with your friends, post and look at photos others have posted. You can keep up to date with friends that live anywhere in the world. You can also play games online and look up lots of websites in areas of interest and research. While this can be good, if you are not aware of how you are using these features there are two factors that can be seriously affected: your health and your safety.

Because it can be fun, it is easy to spend a lot of time in front of the computer or using your phone. In fact, it is easy to get hooked and spend too much time doing this. The time you spend means you have less time for other things that should also be important in your life. Not all of your activities and responsibilities are necessarily fun, but they are still important for your growth and development.

To balance your life, it's important to spend time:

- in face-to-face contact with family and friends (not just online)
- on hobbies such as reading books, playing sport, playing a musical instrument and getting out and about
- helping around the house
- doing homework (if you have it)
- sleeping – everyone needs adequate sleep to function properly.

So, while the internet can be great fun, you should always be in control of how much time you spend on it (or on the phone or watching television, etc.), as well as what you are doing online (i.e. researching an assignment, or socialising in Facebook) to ensure you don't waste time, and make sure you balance 'real-life' things, such as exercise, friends, family, chores, etc.

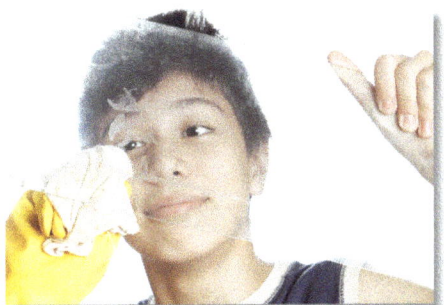

Internet exercise 9

1. Keep a diary for a week that records what you do and how long you spend doing it. Be honest. For time spent on the internet, divide it into:
   a. Socialising (e.g. in chat rooms and on sites like MySpace and YouTube).
   b. Research for schoolwork.
   c. General interest surfing (e.g. the sports pages of a newspaper site)
   d. Playing games.
2. Did you do all your homework?
3. Did you do the tasks/chores in the home you are supposed to?
4. Write a list of things you would like to do, if you had the time.
5. Look at the time you spend on the internet or talking on the phone. What else could you do during this time?
6. What do you think is a reasonable amount of time to spend on the internet each day?

Being cyber smart to stay safe

It would be nice to think that all people can be trusted. The sad fact is that there are many hateful or selfish people purposely trying to trick you and others so they can get something from you or hurt you in some way. These may be people you know or people you don't know. The people you don't know can come from anywhere – next door, the next town or suburb, even the other side of the world.

You can control the effect these people have on you by being aware of what you are doing when you are on the internet or phone, and by being aware of what is going on around you.

- Keep your details, including your real name and where you live, as well as those of your friends and family, private. Always check with your parents or an adult before giving out any personal details.

- It can be a lot of fun making new friends online. Keep in mind that everything is not always as it seems. As you can't see who you are talking to online, that 14-year-old girl you think you are chatting with may in fact be a 50-year-old man pretending.

- You may make new friends online – if you want to meet them, always go with a parent or adult friend, and meet in a busy public place such as a shopping mall or café (rather than a secluded place like a park you know no one ever goes to), to ensure the person you are meeting is who they say they are. The person you think you are friends with may in fact be someone quite different, even dangerous.

- Never give your password to anyone, not even your friends.

- If you feel uncomfortable about something you see on the net or that is sent to you, leave the page or the chat room and don't respond to the message or email. Make sure you tell an adult about it.

- Sites may expect you to fill out forms and include personal details before they enable you to download free items, or register an email address. You should always give the minimum amount of information possible AND check with a parent or adult first. It's often a good idea to have a separate email account set up for such purposes. For example, rather than giving your personal email address (i.e. jackflinders@bigpond.com), where people can see your real name and ISP, create a second email address online (i.e. skaterdude@hotmail.com), which is anonymous, so people can't trace you.

- People may offer you things that seem fantastic and you feel very lucky. These offers will be bogus, another ploy to get information out you that they can use to your detriment. If it seems too good to be true, it probably is.

- If you have a webpage or blog be very careful about the information you put on it. You may think only your friends are reading it, but in reality you may have a much wider audience, as anyone in the world can access it – it is easy to forget and put personal information on. You should also be careful about the photos you load and think about who may be looking at them. In addition to this, you should be considerate of others privacy – never load photos of other people without their consent.

- Treat others as you would like to be treated. Only send the types of messages you would like to receive. Don't write things you would not like other people to write about you.

- Tell someone if you or someone you know is being treated badly.

More on internet safety

www.netalert.gov.au

Netalert is an initiative by the federal government to promote the safe and responsible use of the internet. The site has a huge amount of information that is useful for everyone. Netalert has several other sites that are used for education on internet safety.

www.cybernetrix.com.au

Cybernetrix is a Netalert site. It is fun to use and has lots of information, quizzes and case studies to help you learn about using the internet safely. It looks at chat rooms, mobile phones, being cyber savvy, internet banking scams, identity theft and keeping your computer secure.

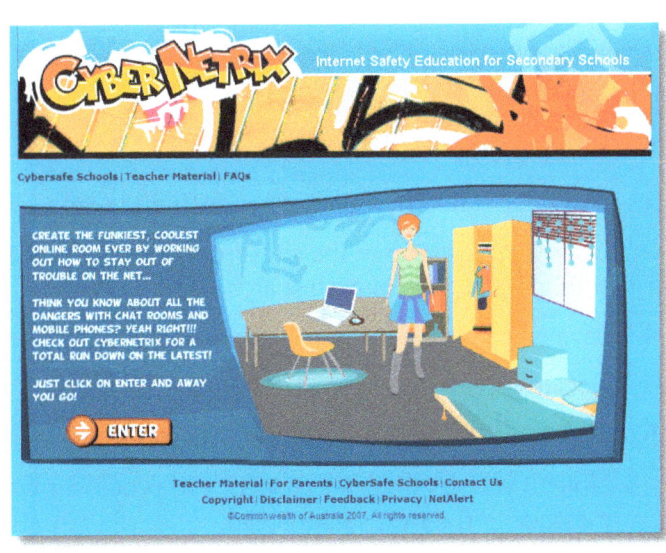

www.wiseuptoit.com.au

Wise Up To It is another site provided by Netalert. This site provides information, advice and stories to help you use the internet safely.

www.chatdanger.com

The Chatdanger site was set up by Childnet International in an effort to provide information and advice on using chatrooms, mobile phones, email, SMS and games safely. Stories and quizzes are also provided. It is bright and easy to use.

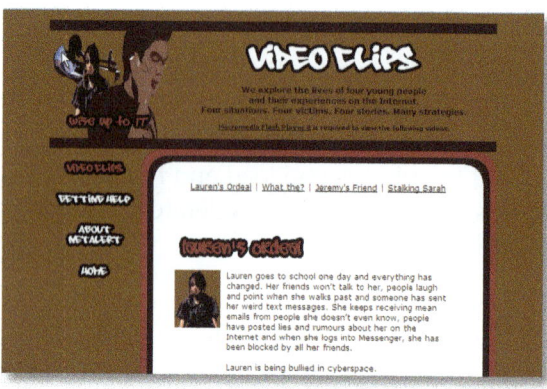

Internet project

1. Pick a topic to research from the following list or choose one of your own but check with your teacher first to make sure it is suitable:
   - a sport you enjoy
   - a type of pet
   - a type of animal
   - a sports person
   - a movie you like
   - a holiday destination
   - an event.

2. Use three different search engines to find some relevant sites.

3. Look up at least 15 of the sites from the results of the searches (i.e. five different sites from the use of each search engine).

4. Save each site in Favorites or Bookmarks.

5. Decide on four sites you think are the best.

6. Make a list of these sites in a word processor file and why you like each of them.

   Note: If you are unable to use a word processor you can list them in the email message in the next step instead.

7. Create a new message to two people in your class, asking them to look up the sites contained in the attached file.

8. Attach the file that contains the list of sites.

9. Send the message to two people in the class and your teacher.

What is word processing?

Word processing is where you use a computer to enter text, make changes to it, record and print it. There are many word processing programs available. The most common one is Microsoft Word.

You use a word processing program to produce professional business letters, reports, poems, song lyrics, job applications, personal resumes, CVs, essays and class projects. A word processor is used anywhere that handwriting could have been used.

Keyboard technique

In order to use word processing packages efficiently, you should try to develop a good keyboard technique. This means using the correct fingers on the keyboard. Your school may have typing books that can be used to improve your keyboard technique, or you may be able to use typing programs such as Mavis Beacon Teaches Typing.

The home keys

Always start with you fingers on the home keys. Most keyboards have markers or raised dots on the **F** and **J** keys. These are there so that you can feel where to place the index finger of each hand without needing to look at the keyboard.

Your left index finger is placed on the **F** key, with the other three fingers on the keys to the left of it: on **D**, **S** and **A**.

Your right index finger is placed on the **J** key, with the other three fingers on the keys to the right of it: on **K**, **L** and **;** (the semi-colon) key.

The other keys

When you need to use the other keys, move the closest finger either up or down. The left index finger can be used to press the **G** key and the right index finger can be used to press the **H** key.

Your thumbs are used to press the **space bar**.

Special keys

Three special keys that are used with word processed documents are the **Shift** key, the **Caps Lock** key and the **Enter** or **return** key.

When entering a document the text should be set to lower case (small letters) with the Caps Lock key set to OFF. When you need to set a letter to upper case (capital letters) such as at the beginning of a sentence or for the name of a place or person, hold down the Shift key and press the letter.

If you need to type a heading in upper case, turn the Caps Lock key on to type the word or words then turn the Caps Lock key back off for the rest of the text.

The Enter or Return key is only used at the end of a paragraph, the end of a heading or to leave a blank line.

Correct posture

It is important to be seated correctly in front of the computer screen. This will reduce tiredness and place less stress on your arms and back.

- Your body should be in line with the centre of the computer screen.
- Your eyes should be level with the computer screen.
- Your feet should be flat on the floor.

Entering a document

When entering a document, all the words should be entered first in plain text. Once all the text has been entered, corrections and formatting can be conducted.

As noted, the Enter or Return key is only pressed to:

- complete a paragraph
- complete a heading
- leave a blank line.

Unlike typewriters, in computer word processing you never need to press the Enter or Return key at the end of a line, as the text will roll onto the next line automatically. This process is called **word wrap**.

Word processing exercise 1

Skills practised:

Entering text

Editing

Using the Enter key

Saving

Paragraph setting

Spell checking

Using the Caps Lock key

Revision – Entering a document

To revise the correct way to produce a document, enter the business letter shown below.
To do this efficiently you should use the following steps:

1. Enter all the text first without any formats.
2. Have the Caps Lock key set to OFF and hold down the Shift key and type the letter when you need a capital letter.
3. Press the Enter or Return key only when indicated.

25 March 2010	\<enter\>
	press \<enter\> 4 times
Mrs Leanne Forrest	\<enter\>
202 Hyatt Street	\<enter\>
Bendigo Vic 3550	\<enter\>
	\<enter\>
Dear Leanne	\<enter\>
	\<enter\>

I congratulate you on winning first prize in our national raffle. You are now the proud owner of a BMW 318i Automatic Sedan valued at $56,170. This includes all on-road costs. \<enter\>

\<enter\>

We would like to invite you to our office at 66 Jules Court, Carlton, 3053 on 1 April 2010 so that the presentation of the car can be made to you. Please feel free to bring your family members with you. \<enter\>

\<enter\>

Yours sincerely	\<enter\>
	press \<enter\> 4 times
Shaun O'Farrell	\<enter\>
Hearing Research Centre	\<enter\>

4. Once complete, save the document in your storage folder under an appropriate name, such as **WP Exercise 1**.
5. Spell check the document then **Print Preview** it.
6. Carefully read through the preview and correct any errors. If you have difficulty proofreading from the screen, print a copy, mark any errors with a pen then correct the errors on the screen.
7. After the corrections have been made to the document, resave it by pressing **Ctrl+S** or ⌘**+S** and print a final copy.

Formatting text

Text can be set to a variety of appearances. The process of altering the appearance of text is called **formatting**. You can set text to **bold**, *italic* or underline when you need it to stand out.

The best time to format text is after you have finished entering it (typed it in). To format text, highlight the word or section of text, then click the appropriate button in the toolbar (such as *I* for italic), or click on **Font** within the Format menu.

If you format text as you enter it, you have to keep turning the formatting off and on as you go, which can slow you down and may create errors. It's more logical and efficient to type in the text first, then create the formatting second.

Word processing exercise 2

Formatting text

1. Load your letter from the previous exercise (if it is not already open). We will add some text and formats to it.
2. Position the cursor at the beginning of the first line (just before the date at the top of the letter).
3. Enter the heading: HEARING RESEARCH CENTRE
4. Press the Enter key five times: once to complete the heading and the other four times to leave four blank lines.
5. Highlight all of the heading and set:
   - the Font to Century School Book or Times New Roman
   - the Font Size to 18 point
   - the Font Style to Bold and Shadow (if available)
   - and the Alignment to Centre.
6. Highlight the words: BMW 318i Automatic Sedan and set their format to Italic.
7. Highlight the price: $56,170 and set its format to bold.

Your letter should look like the one displayed on the opposite page.

Skills practised:

Entering text

Editing

Using the Enter key

Saving

Paragraph setting

Spell checking

Printing

Hearing Research Centre

25 March 2010

Mrs Leanne Forrest
202 Hyatt Street
Bendigo Vic 3550

Dear Leanne

I congratulate you on winning first prize in our national raffle. You are now the proud owner of a *BMW 318i Automatic Sedan* valued at **$56,170**. This includes all on-road costs.

We would like to invite you to our office at 66 Jules Court, Carlton, 3053 on 1 April 2010 so that the presentation of the car can be made to you. Please feel free to bring your family members with you.

Yours sincerely

Shaun O'Farrell
Hearing Research Centre

8. Save the document on your storage disk or flash drive, or in your storage folder.
9. Spell check the document then Print Preview it.
10. Carefully read through the preview and correct any errors. If you have difficulty proofreading from the screen, print a copy, mark any errors with a pen then correct the errors on the screen.
11. After the corrections have been made to the document, resave it by pressing **Ctrl+S** or **⌘+S** and print a final copy.

Copying and pasting text

You can copy text and paste it to other sections of a document. This saves you the effort of re-entering text. When you wish to simply move text you can **cut** it from the screen and **paste** it at the required position.

To see an example of copying and pasting you will be entering the song lyrics from the theme song of the film *Fly Away Home*. The song has a chorus, which should only be entered once.

Word processing exercise 3

Skills practised:

Entering text

Editing

Copy and paste

Formatting text

Copying and pasting text

Enter the song lyrics shown below. To do this efficiently you should follow these steps:

1. Enter all the text first without any formats.
2. Press Enter at the end of each line, and leave two lines after the heading and before the songwriter's name.
3. Format the heading after all the text has been entered to be **Bold** and **Shadow** (if available).
4. Highlight the chorus heading and set it to *Italic*.

10,000 Miles

Farewell my own true love.
Farewell for a while.
I'm going away, but I'll be back
Though I go 10,000 miles.

Chorus
10,000 miles, my own true love
10,000 miles or more.
The rocks may melt and the seas may burn
If I should not return.

Oh come ye back my own true love
And stay a while with me.
If I had a friend on this earth
You've been a friend to me.

Traditional

5. Highlight the chorus, including its heading, and press **Ctrl**+**C** or ⌘+**C** to copy it.
6. Set the cursor at the blank line just above 'Traditional' and paste the chorus by pressing **Ctrl**+**V** or ⌘+**V**.
7. Press Enter to leave an extra blank line before the word 'Traditional'.
8. Save the document on your storage disk or flash drive, or in your storage folder.
9. Spell check the document then Print Preview it.
10. Carefully read through the preview and correct any errors. If you have difficulty proofreading from the screen, print a copy, mark any errors with a pen then correct the errors on the screen.
11. After the corrections have been made to the document, resave it by pressing **Ctrl**+**S** or ⌘+**S** and print a final copy.

Inserting page breaks and moving text

Many documents you create have more than one page. You need to be able to format those pages. This includes setting **page breaks**, which finishes the page and takes the cursor to the top of the next page, and adding **page numbers**, which places the number of the page at the bottom of the page. You can even copy text from one page to another.

In the next exercise you will adjust the song lyrics you entered in the last exercise by copying them to a second page, inserting page numbers and moving text in the copied version of the song.

Word processing exercise 4

Inserting page breaks and moving text
1. Load the song lyrics from exercise 3.
2. Highlight the whole song by choosing Select from the Editing group of the ribbon (Toolbar).
3. Place the cursor at the end of the document (after 'Traditional') and Insert a page break using Page Break from the Pages group of the Insert tab in the ribbon.
4. Paste the song onto the second page.
5. From the Header and Footer group of the Insert tab use the Page Number icon to insert page numbers at the bottom of centre of each page.
6. Close the Header and Footer screen by clicking on the Close Header and Footer icon at the right of the ribbon.
7. Highlight the first verse and cut it from the screen.

Skills practised:

Editing

Copy and paste (moving text)

Inserting page breaks

Inserting page numbers

Using find and replace

8 Set the cursor at the beginning of the second verse and paste the first verse.
9 Repeat step 8 to place the second verse where the first was. The song on the second page should look like the one shown below.

10,000 Miles

Oh come ye back my own true love
And stay a while with me.
If I had a friend all on this earth
You've been a friend to me.

Chorus
10,000 miles, my own true love
10,000 miles or more.
The rocks may melt and the seas may burn
If I should not return.

Fare thee well my own true love.
Farewell for a while.
I'm going away, but I'll be back
Though I go 10,000 miles.

Chorus
10,000 miles, my own true love
10,000 miles or more.
The rocks may melt and the seas may burn
If I should not return.

Traditional

10 Use **Save As** from the **File** menu to Save the document under a different name from the one you used in the last exercise such as **WP exericse 4**.
11 Check over the document and make any adjustments.
12 Use the Replace icon from the Editing group of the Home tab to change all the occurrences of the word 'rocks' with 'cliffs' in the copy on the second page only.
13 Print a final copy of your two pages.

Tab stops

When you need to align text within a document, **tab stops** must be set. The space bar should never be used, as the text will not print straight because not all the letters are of equal width.

Tab stops can be set in the program's **ruler**. When you press the **Tab** key, the cursor will jump to the set tab stop. These set tab stops can be adjusted using the **Format** menu and any text set to them will be adjusted as well. There are four main types of tab stops, which align the text to the **Left**, **Right**, **Centre** or to **Decimal** points.

> ∟ Represents a left justified tab.
> ┴ Represents a centre justified tab.
> ⌐ Represents a right justified tab.
> ┴. Represents a decimal justified tab.

Word processing exercise 5

Tab stops

Follow these steps to enter the table shown below.

1. The main heading should be Bold and 14 point.
2. For the sub-headings set **centre justified tab stops** for the second and third sub-headings.
3. For the items in the table set Decimal tab stops in line with the headings.

Skills practised:

Tab stops

Left aligned tabs

Centre aligned tabs

Right aligned tabs

Decimal tabs

Rock Star Earnings, 2009

Performer	Record sales $millions	Royalties $millions
Elton John	4.57	11.75
Justin Timberlake	11.34	23.86
Kylie Minogue	3.93	8.41
Beyoncé	7.66	13.75

4. Once complete, save the document on your storage disk or flash drive, or in your storage folder.
5. Check over the document and make any adjustments. Resave the table if you made any changes.
6. Print a copy of the document.

Page margins and indents

Page margins

Page margins are the spaces between the edge of the paper and where your text is printed. They allow you to control where your text is printed on a page. All printers require a certain amount of space from the edge of the paper to where the printing starts, as documents would not look very professional if they started very close to the edge of the paper. The diagram shows the position of the page margins.

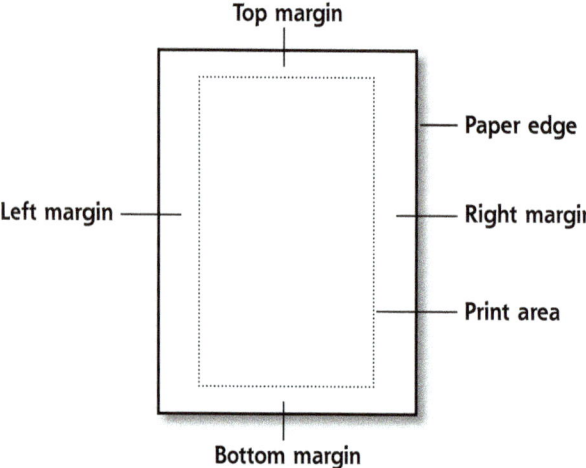

Setting page margins

When you need to adjust the width of paragraphs within a page, the **indent markers** in the **ruler** are used. The indent markers are the solid triangles at both ends of the ruler. The following diagram indicates what the markers represent.

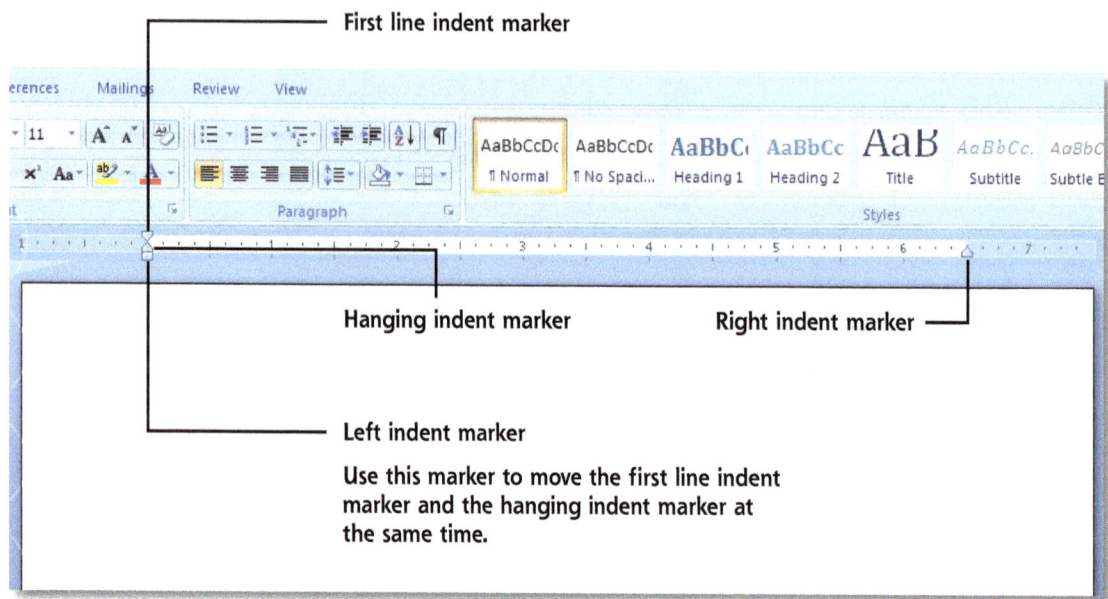

Word processing exercise 6

Skills practised:

Setting margins

Setting indents

Setting page margins

1. Use the Margins icon in the Page Layout tab to set the margins to Normal.
   Each margin will be set to 2.54 cm.
2. Enter the following document without any formatting.

MUSIC ONLINE

Music Online will be demonstrated at the 'Music World Wide' show, which is to be held at Auckland's Superdrome from 29 November. This is the first time the highly successful exhibition has been held in New Zealand. Previous shows have been held in Adelaide, Melbourne, Sydney, Perth and Brisbane.

According to Exhibition Manager, Tania Harris:

    'The exhibition in Auckland is shaping up to be an outstanding success. The involvement of Music Online will be a major boost.'

A report just completed by the Australian Retail Sales Association has concluded that:

    'Purchasing music over the internet is the fastest growing sales area in Australia and New Zealand.'

It is estimated that there are well in excess of 1 million Australians and New Zealanders who have purchased music over the internet in the past year through Music Online.

3. Once all the text has been entered, format the heading as bold caps.
4. Highlight the paragraph that starts 'The exhibition in Auckland ...' and move its left indent marker to 1 cm and its right indent marker to 13 cm.
5. Repeat step 3 for the paragraph that starts 'Purchasing music over the internet ...'
6. Once complete, save the document on your storage disk or flash drive, or in your storage folder.
7. Spell check the document then carefully proofread it.
8. Make the corrections to the document, resave it and print a copy.

MODULE 2

Combining tabs and indents

Tab stops and indents can be used together in the production of documents. This can be very useful when you need to create **hanging indents**, which set indented text to be in line. For example, the instructions in this book use hanging indents.

5   Highlight all of the text and set the **font** to **Times New Roman**, the **font size** to
    18 point and the **style** to **bold**.

    ← hanging indent

Word processing exercise 7

Combining tabs and indents

Create the personality profile shown below. You can insert your own details if you wish.

1 You will need to set a **right justified tab stop** for the titles and set the **left indent** (or hanging indent) marker for the responses.
2 Carry out the formats once all the text has been entered.

Skills practised:

Entering text

Editing

Formatting

Using tabs stops

Using indents

PERSONALITY PROFILE

Name:	Julie Robinson
Celebrity status:	Miss Universe 2010
Date of birth:	30 September 1990
Brothers and sisters:	2 (not counting Stuart)
Pets:	Cat called Nicky; dog called Paris
Favourite food:	Pizza with chips
Favourite drink:	Lemon and lime with ginger ale
Favourite group:	The Black Eyed Peas
Favourite car:	Lada
Likes:	Rodney, movies, Rodney, dancing, Rodney, netball, Rodney, shopping, Rodney, football.
Dislikes:	Loud or self-centred people, Julia, Science, Julia, washing dishes.
Ambition:	To be rich and famous, married to Rodney with 10 children, 2 cats, a dog and a canary.

3 Once complete, save the document in your storage folder.
4 Spell check the document then carefully proofread it.
5 Make the corrections to the document, resave it and print a copy.

Further tabs and indents

To practise the use of tab stops and indents you will produce the memo shown below. You will need to use the ruler carefully.

Word processing exercise 8

Further tabs and indents

1 For the **Date** to **Subject** section, set a right justified tab stop for the sub-headings and move the left (or hanging) indent marker for the responses.

2 For the paragraphs, set the left indent and first line indent markers to the position where you want the left edges to start (in line with the responses).

3 The company name should be centred, set to bold and the font size increased.

4 The address should be centred and the same font size as the rest of the document.

5 The sub-headings **Date:**, **To:**, etc. need to be entered and set to bold.

Skills practised:

Entering text

Editing

Formatting

Using tabs stops

Using indents

Sam's Pizza Palace

180 Gibson Street, Canterbury, 2193

Date: 14 October 2010

To: Sam Alterini
Title: Manager/Owner

From: Ronald O'Reilly
Title: Pizza Maker

Subject: The advertised position of waiter.

I would like to apply for the recently advertised waiter position.

I have been making pizzas for you for seven years.
This has given me extensive knowledge of our product line.
I believe that I am well presented and would like to have more contact with the public.

Could an interview be arranged at your convenience?
Thank you for your consideration.

6 Once complete, save the document on your storage disk or flash drive, or in your storage folder.

7 Spell check the document then carefully proofread it.

8 Make the corrections to the document, resave it and print a copy.

Bulleted and numbered lists

An application of hanging indents is the use of bulleted or numbered lists. Most modern word processing programs have automated the process of creating these types of lists.

Word processing exercise 9

Skills practised:

Using bullets

Formatting bullets

Numbered lists

Bulleted and numbered lists

1. Enter the following text:

   COOKING TIPS <enter>
   <enter>
   Here are a few cooking tips that may be worth referring to when preparing the recipes in this book: <enter>
   <enter>
   Always try to cook vegetables by steaming. If you do not have a steamer, wrap the vegetable in foil and cook them in an oven. <enter>
   <enter>
   Always clean vegetables before cooking. A nail brush can be useful to clean vegetables that do not need the skin removed. <enter>
   <enter>
   Try not to over-cook food. A cooked vegetable should be firm, not hard or soft. Fish is cooked when its flesh is white and fine and can be broken easily. <enter>

2. Highlight the text from 'Always try to cook vegetables by steaming' to the end of the document.
3. Set the text to a bullet, and the hanging indent should be automatically set.
4. Highlight the three bulleted points and change the format of the bullet to another symbol such as a tick. Refer to the text below as an example.

COOKING TIPS

Here are a few cooking tips that may be worth referring to when preparing the recipes in this book:

- ✓ Always try to cook vegetables by steaming. If you do not have a steamer, wrap the vegetable in foil and cook them in an oven.
- ✓ Always clean vegetables before cooking. A nail brush can be useful to clean vegetables that do not need the skin removed.
- ✓ Try not to over-cook food. A cooked vegetable should be firm, not hard or soft. Fish is cooked when its flesh is white and fine and can be broken easily.

5 Highlight the three bulleted points and change the text to a numbered list, for example:

COOKING TIPS

Here are a few cooking tips that may be worth referring to when preparing the recipes in this book:

1 Always try to cook vegetables by steaming. If you do not have a steamer, wrap the vegetable in foil and cook them in an oven.

2 Always clean vegetables before cooking. A nail brush can be useful to clean vegetables that do not need the skin removed.

3 Try not to over-cook food. A cooked vegetable should be firm, not hard or soft. Fish is cooked when its flesh is white and fine and can be broken easily.

6 Save the document and print a copy if you wish.

Leader characters

Leader characters fill the space before **tab stops** with dots, dashes or underlines. They are a neat way of underlining tables or aligning numbers to text in a contents page.

Word processing exercise 10

Leader characters

Create the contents page for a cookbook.

1 Enter the text from the following page without formatting it.

2 For the contents items set a **right justified tab stop** at the right of the ruler, double click on the tab stop in the ruler and set to have a **dotted leader character**.

Note: The right justified tab stop ensures that the right edge of the page numbers are in line.

3 Once all the text has been entered, format the headings and increase the font size of the contents items if you wish.

Skills practised:

Right aligned tab stops

Leader characters

NAN'S FAVOURITES

CONTENTS

Introduction	vii
Ingredients required	1
Cooking tips	3
Starters	4
Soups	10
Salads	15
Main dishes	21
Pasta and rice	46
Desserts	52
Drinks	60
Index	72

4 Once complete, save the document to your storage disk or flash drive, or in your storage folder.

5 Spell check the document then **Print Preview** it.

6 Carefully read through the preview and correct any errors. If you have difficulty proofreading from the screen, print a copy, mark any errors with a pen then correct the errors on the screen.

7 After corrections have been made to the document, resave it by pressing **Ctrl+S** or ⌘**+S** and print a final copy.

Further tabs and indents

To practise the use of tab stops and indents you will produce the opposite business letter. You will need to use the **ruler** carefully.

Word processing exercise 11

Further tabs and indents

1 Enter the text of the letter without any formatting.

2 For the first table, set three **centre justified tab stops** for the headings.

3 For the fees in the table, set a **left justified tab stop**. For the values set two **decimal tab stops**.

4 For the membership application form, set a **left justified tab stop** at the right of the ruler and set this tab stop to have a **leader character**.

Skills practised:

Tab stops

Leader characters

Indents

5 As extra sections are needed in the application form, set more left justified tab stops and set them to have the same leader character.
6 Spell check the document, print a copy, proofread the document and make any adjustments.
7 Print another copy if you made any changes.

MANICURE GOLF CLUB
35 Green Grass Road, Sandringham Vic 3191

<today's date>

Mr Anthony Mercuri
24 Austin Crescent
Frankston Vic 3199

Dear Mr Mercuri

Thank you for your inquiry about joining the Manicure Golf Club. We believe the club is one of the finest in the area and we certainly welcome new members. Our rates are listed in the following table:

Fee	Normal rate	Pensioner rate
Joining fee	$1050.00	$535.00
Yearly membership	$825.00	$295.00
Associate membership	$525.00	$95.00

Please detach and complete the membership application form at the bottom of this letter and send it to the club president.

Yours faithfully

Peter McLean
Secretary

MEMBERSHIP APPLICATION FORM
Surname Ms /Mrs / Miss / Mr ....
Given names ....
Home address ....
   .... Postcode ....
Telephone: Business (....) ....   Home (....) ....
Nominated by ....

Page formats

Formatting pages involves such things as setting the page into **columns** or adding **headers** and **footers**.

Pages can be set to display text in multiple **columns**. The text flows down the first column then down the second column, etc.

At the top of each page there is a section set aside for a **header**. Text or graphics set in the header section are displayed at the top of each page.

At the bottom of each page there is a section set aside for a **footer**. Text or graphics set in the footer section are displayed at the bottom of each page.

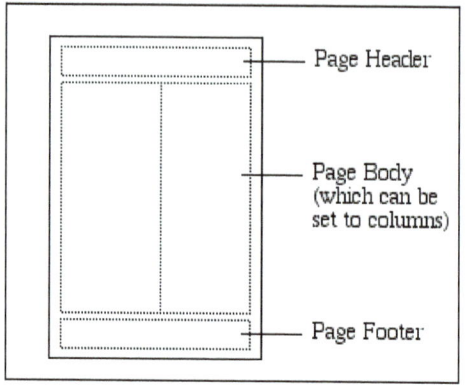

Word processing exercise 12

Page formats

Create the newsletter shown below.

1. Format the text into two columns and justify the text.
2. Add a header and footer.

Skills practised:

Entering text

Editing

Formatting

Columns

Headers and footers

LISMORE LIBRARY GAZETTE

Volume 2   June, 2010

Your Community Library

As part of the Free Public Library Service, your Lismore Community Library welcomes you to avail yourself of its facilities. Membership is FREE and it costs nothing to borrow a book. To enroll simply complete an application form and provide proof of address, and you will be given a Free Membership Card. This card can be used to borrow books from any of the Regional Library branches. There is no limit to the number of books you can borrow, but we do ask that you borrow no more than two books on the same subject. Up to four magazines may be borrowed.

Finding a Good Book

The Lismore Library is fully automated with three public access terminals providing speedy access to books and periodicals, either by title, author or subject. The catalogue is online to the other regional libraries, so if the book is not available at Lismore, it can be reserved from the other regional branches. If you have a fear of technology, the old card catalogue system still remains. Help is always available from the librarians simply by asking at the Advisor's Desk.

Share Your Reading

The Lismore Book Club has been in operation for over a year now and its membership has been steadily growing. New members are most welcome – it is open to anyone who wishes to participate. Meetings are held once a month, with members expected to provide a review of a book they have read that month. As well, discussions about topical books are conducted, reading strategies arranged and suggestions about future reading made. The aim of the club is to encourage people to read more and to share their experiences. If you would like to join the growing band of avid readers, please contact the Library staff.

Myth, Legend or Fact?

The Loch Ness Monster has fascinated people for centuries. Sightings and photographs have constantly surfaced, yet no one has convinced the sceptics of the monster's existence. At last there is a book that says it has the answers. It's called *The Truth About Lochy* by Arthur Robinson. We won't spoil your curiosity by telling you what conclusions the author has made – let's just say you will be pleasantly surprised.

The Lismore Community Library
Kresta Road, Lismore, 3324

3 Save the document on your storage disk or flash drive, or in your storage folder.
4 Spell check the document then carefully proofread it.
5 Make the corrections to the document, resave it and print a copy.

Inserting graphics

Most modern word-processing programs allow for graphics in the form of pictures, photographs or video clips to be added to documents. This can enhance the appearance of the document. The program may have its own clip art library of sketches or your school may have a library of graphics that you can use in you documents. You can even scan graphics and insert them if necessary.

To illustrate the use of graphics, you will produce the flyer for a jazz cafe shown below. If you haven't used the Microsoft Drawing Tools before, your teacher may want you to work though the Microsoft Office Drawing Tools Module before starting this activity.

Word processing exercise 13

Inserting graphics

1 You can use WordArt for the main heading, or set the text to Shadow and Outline.
2 The Clip Art sketches can be found in the Music section of the Microsoft Clip Gallery or you can substitute graphics from your school's graphics library.

Skills practised:

Entering text

Editing

Formatting

Inserting graphics

Formatting graphics

Grand Opening

Jazz Cafe

A new, modern cafe in the heart of Frankston, offering a wide selection of meals at reasonable prices, with romantic settings and a live jazz band playing each night.

Bookings for clubs and groups available.

Emma's Jazz Cafe
24 Morris Street, Frankston, 3199
For information call (03) 9781 2907

3. Save the document on your storage disk or flash drive, or in your storage folder.
4. Spell check the document then carefully proofread it.
5. Make the corrections to the document, resave it and print a copy.

Multiple page documents

When headers and footers are used in a document, you often don't want them displayed on the first page. This page might be a **title page** that introduces the document.

Headers and footers can be turned off completely, or from the first page of a document only – not randomly throughout the document.

To illustrate this you will create a two-page recipe shown below and opposite. The first page will be a **title page** with a graphic. The recipe itself is on the next page. It will require the use of **hanging indents** and a **header**.

Word processing exercise 14

Skills practised:

Formatting text

Inserting graphics

Formatting graphics

Using page borders

Creating a title page

Inserting footnotes

Multiple page documents

1. Enter the text for the title (or first) page.
2. Insert an appropriate graphic on the title page and add a page border.

— page break —

3. Insert a page break and enter the recipe. You will need to set the title of the recipe in the header section.
4. Set the document so that the headers and footers are not displayed on the title page.
5. Add the following footnotes to the recipe (footnotes are references displayed at either the bottom of a page or at the end of a document): 50 g = 2 oz
   300 ml = 0.5 pt
   180°C = 350°F

CONTINENTAL CHEESE CAKE

Ingredients (metric measurements)

Base

50 g caster sugar
50 g self-raising flour
50 g margarine

15 g baking powder
1 egg

Filling

500 g cream cheese
300 ml double cream
75 g margarine
50 g caster sugar

50 g plain flour
1 egg
1 lemon, juice and rind
50 g sultanas

Method

1. In a large bowl mix together all the ingredients for the base. Spread on the base of a greased 23 cm tin.
2. Work the cream cheese until smooth, add in the cream and beat together.
3. Cream the margarine, sugar and lemon rind together in another bowl until smooth. Gradually add the flour, lemon juice and rind, egg and sultanas.
4. Fold in the cheese and cream mixture and mix until smooth.
5. Pour on top of the base mixture in the tin. Bake at 180°C for $1\frac{1}{4}$ to $1\frac{1}{2}$ hours. Allow to cool. Remove the tin and chill.

   50 g = 2 oz
   300 ml = 0.5 pt
   180°C = 350°F

6. Save the document on your storage disk or flash drive, or in your storage folder.
7. Spell check the document, print a copy, proofread it, make any adjustments then resave.
8. Print a final copy of your two pages.

Using sections

There are times when you want part of a page formatted in one way and other parts of the same page formatted differently. For example, you might want part of a page to have text in three columns and other parts of the page to have a single column. Sections allow you to do this.

MODULE 2

Word processing exercise 15

In this exercise you will create an advertising page for a used car company. It will need sections to be inserted throughout the page. The text and image can be inserted from the PIT Book 1 Support Files, which can be downloaded from the Cambridge website (www.cambridge.edu.au/education/PIT). You might need to ask your teacher for the location of the files.

1. Access the **PIT Book 1 Support Files**, open the **Word processing** folder then open the **WP exercise 15** folder.
2. Open the **WP exercise 15** document.
   Your task will be to format the page shown as follows. Start by formatting the main headings and use the Drawing Tools to shade them.
3. Centre the Small Cars sub-heading and format it.
4. Position the cursor at the beginning of the first small car, '00 Astra Olympic', and insert a Continuous Section Break by clicking on the Breaks icon in the Page Layout tab and selecting Continuous.
5. Use the Columns icon in the Page Layout tab to set the page to two columns. This will only occur in the new section.
6. Set another Continuous Section Break at the beginning of the Family Cars sub-heading. Set the Columns back to one then centre the sub-heading and format it in the same way as you did for the Small Cars sub-heading. Remember, you can use the Format Painter tool.
7. Repeat steps 4 to 6 for the rest of the family cars and sports car text.
8. In the blank line after the last sports car insert another Continuous Section Break and set the columns back to one.
9. Insert the CAR picture from the WP Exercise 15 folder. Reduce the size of the picture so that it fits neatly under the text and centre it.
10. Format the name of each car in the columns to italic.
11. Open the Header view by clicking on the Header icon in the Insert tab and selecting Edit Header.
12. Use the Shapes icon from the Insert tab to add a rectangle around the page.
13. Select the Header and Footer Tools at the top of the ribbon and select the Close Header and Footer icon to return to the normal screen.
14. Check over the document then print a copy of your finished product.

Skills practised:

Sections

Section breaks

Columns

Column breaks

Inserting an image

Formatting an image

Header and footer

Drawing tools

Honest Andy's Quality Used Cars

Small Cars

00 Astra Olympic, $17,990
EFI, 5-speed, air-con, p/steering, dual airbags, one owner, 125,000 km.

'01 Honda Civic GLi, $8,990
Automatic, air-con, p/steering, airbag, electric windows, 77,000 km.

'99 Hyundai Excel, $3,990
5-speed, air-con, p/steering 15" alloys, CD player, 90,000 km.

'98 Toyota Seca RV, $5,990
1.8 l. EFI, 5-speed, air-con, p/steering, alloys, 95,000 km.

Family Cars

'03 Toyota Camry CSi, $14,990
V6 automatic, air-con, p/steering, cruise control, one owner, 19,000 km.

'03 Ford AU XR-6, $18,990
Automatic, air-con, p/steering, cruise control, one owner, 72,000 km.

'01 Holden VT Exec II, $16,990
airbag, V6 automatic, air-con, p/steering, control, remote locking, 85,000 km.

'04 TJ Magna Executive, $18,990
3.5 l. MPFI, auto, air-con, p/steering, cruise control, CD player, 97,000 km.

Sports Cars

'03 Subaru Impreza WRX, $24,990
2.0 l. turbo, 5-speed, air-con, p/steering, airbag, ABS brakes, one owner, 93,000 km.

'02 Toyota Celica SX, $16,990
1.8 l. EEFi, 6-speed, air-con, p/steering, cruise control, alloys, one owner, 82,000 km.

'99 Honda Prelude, $7,990
2.0 l. VTEC, auto, air-con, p/steering, cruise control, central locking, red, 105,000 km.

'93 Mazda MX6 Coupe, $9,990
2.5 l. V6, auto, sunroof, air-con, p/steering, cruise control, CD player, 197,000 km.

MODULE 2

word processing

MODULE 2

A more detailed newsletter

Sections allow you to produce quite complex documents, as the following exercise demonstrates. In this exercise you will create a newsletter for a travel agency. It will need sections to be inserted. The text and images can be inserted from the PIT Book 1 Support Files, which can be downloaded from the Cambridge University Press website (www.cambridge.edu.au/education/PIT). You might need to ask your teacher for the location of the files.

Word processing exercise 16

A more detailed newsletter

1. Access the Pit Book 1 Support Files, open the Word Processing folder followed by the WP Exercise 16 folder. And open the WP Exercise 16 document.

   Your task will be to format the page as shown on the following page.

2. Start by formatting the main heading and use the Drawing Tools to shade it.

3. Set at right tab stop at the right edge of the ruler for the second line (Issue 4 …).

4. Format the 'May Madness Again, Cut Price Tours to Europe' lines to bold and larger then add horizontal lines above and below them.

5. Insert a Continuous Section Break at the beginning of the line 'Due to the success …' then format the section to three columns with a 0.5 cm column spacing using the Columns icon in the ribbon and selecting More Columns.

6. Insert another Continuous Section Break at the beginning of the sub-heading 'Contents', set the columns back to one and press Enter or Return to add a blank line above the Contents.

7. At the first blank line after the Brisbane phone number, insert the Big Ben picture from the WP Exerise 16 folder using the Picture icon from the Insert tab of the ribbon.

8. Format the text in the three columns to be full justified and adjust the font size so that the text fills the first two columns.

9. Add a left tab stop to the Melbourne, Sydney and Brisbane lines at the end of the second column so that the phone number is in line.

10. If you have room, use a text box to add a caption below the Big Ben picture that says 'London tours become very popular at this time of year'. Format the caption text to italic and turn off the text box border.

11. Position the cursor at the beginning of the Contents sub-heading and insert the Venice picture from the WP Exercise 16 folder.

Skills practised:

Sections

Columns

Continuous section break

Drawing tools

Justifying text

Inserting images

Formatting images

Tab stops

Leader characters

Page borders

12 Reduce the size of the picture to 50% and set its Text Wrapping icon (Arrange group in the Format tab of the ribbon) to Tight so that the Contents text is to the right of the picture.

13 Set the four sections of the Contents to have a right tab stop and dotted leader characters (double click on the tab stop to do this). If you wish you can cut the five lines of the Contents section, paste them into a text box next to the Venice picture, then shade the text box and format the text.

14 Add a rectangle around the page in the Header view.

15 Check over the document then print a copy of your finished product.

Madigan's Travel

Issue 4   April, 2005

May Madness Again, Cut Price Tours to Europe

Due to the success of last year's May promotion, we have decided to repeat the offer this year. We have again cut the prices of all our May European tours. May is the best time to visit Europe: summer is fast approaching and the tourist season of June to August hasn't quite started.

In this newsletter we will describe the European destinations that we can provide. You can also contact us if you would like us to customise your tour. Whether you want the old world charm of England, the vitality of Italy or the hospitality of Germany, we have the tour for you. You can stay in 5-star hotels, or quaint bed-and-breakfast inns. All your needs are catered for by our experienced couriers who ensure that your tour is enjoyable and trouble free.

Our tours start between 5 May and 10 May, so don't delay your booking. There are limited places and last year they sold out before the end of April!

Your can contact our agents at:
Melbourne   (03) 6310 3622
Sydney   (02) 2213 0241
Brisbane   (07) 8382 5900

London tours become very popular at this time of year.

CONTENTS:
England, Scotland, Ireland........................ 2
France, Italy, Greece 4
Norway, Sweden, Demark 6
Germany, Austria, Poland........................ 8

Word processing project

You are the manager of Emma's Jazz Café, which specialises in fine seafood served to fine music. Up until now, a local printer has produced the menus. The problem is that the menus are constantly changing due to the seasonal availability of certain foods, resulting in the cost of constantly updating the menus becoming too high.

You have decided to produce the menus within the café and update them as required. You need the first menu created. The text can be downloaded from the PIT Book 1 Support Files on the Cambridge University Press website (www.cambridge.edu.au/education/PIT). The file is called **WP Project Text**. The menu will need to be two pages, which can be printed back to back then placed on tables. It will be up to you to find appropriate graphics from **Clip Art** and decide on the appropriate format for the data.

Collect the data

Plan the format your publication will take (newsletter, flyer and number of columns, etc.) and work out what graphics you will need to collect (check the **Clip Art**).

Design the solution

Draw thumbnail sketches for each page of your publication. Include what fonts and styles you are going to use, columns and tab types and where the graphics will be placed, etc. The following diagrams show examples of the planning you should do.

A   If there are differently formatted pages in your document, draw a Structure Diagram to indicate the different pages, for example, for a cookbook:

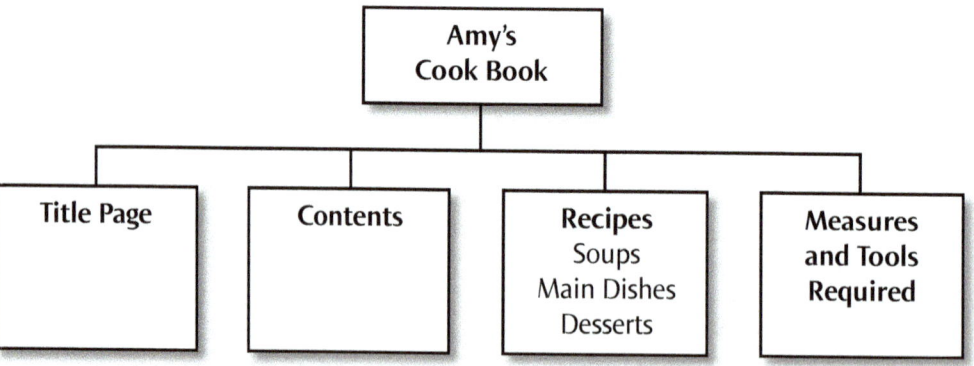

B   Draw a detailed layout (or mock-up) diagram to show how each different page will look. The diagram should include the format of the text – headings, sub-heading and text body, any images to be inserted or drawing tools to be used, etc. For example:

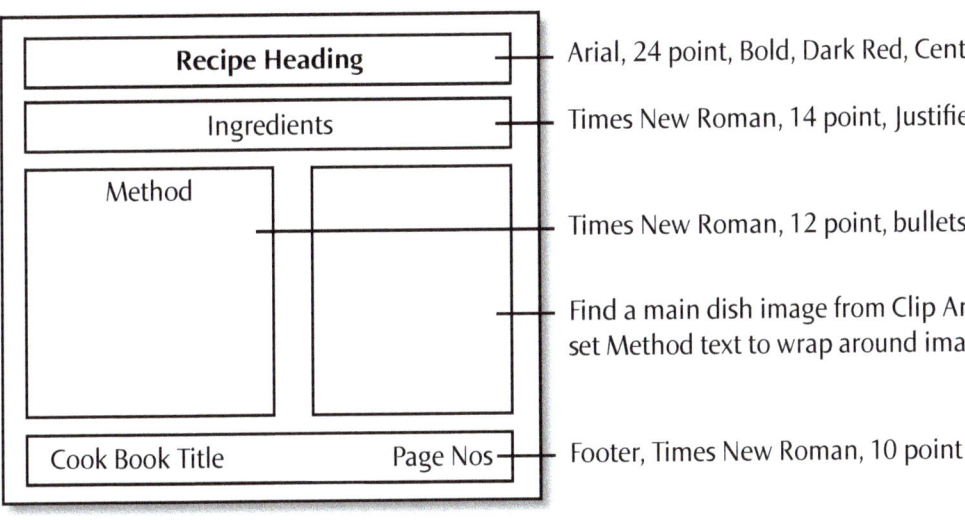

Produce the solution

Use your word processing skills to produce the solution and print a copy of it.

Evaluate the solution

1. Ask other people to look at your publication and give you feedback on the quality and accuracy of your publication. Describe what was said and the changes you made to your document because of their comments.
2. How will your solution make the operation of the Emma's Jazz Café easier in the future?

Café Data

Emma's Jazz Café

A restaurant of fine seafood served to fine music. Only organic ingredients are used.

Open 7:00 am – 11:00 pm 7 days
666 Brunswick Street, Fitzroy 3065
Phone	(03) 9417 9007
Fax	(03) 9417 9008
Email	orders@emmas.com.au
Web	www.emmas.com.au

Appetisers

Seafood and Avocado Cocktail $5.25
Avocado overflowing with deep sea scallops and green prawns.

Sardines in a Crust $5.95
Deliciously crisp served with lemon wedges.

Calamari $7.80
Deep fried to perfection with a zesty Italian sauce.

Oysters Rockefeller $8.30
Half a dozen oysters topped with traditional spinach sauce.

Crab in Parsley Crepes $6.75
Lightly curried and generously filled.

Mushroom Mousse $4.30
Gently pureed with walnuts and lemon.

Salads & Soups

Roman Salad $3.00
A blend of romaine lettuce, seasoned croutons, anchovies, eggs and grated parmesan.

Crunchy Spinach Salad $2.55
Fresh young spinach leaves topped with avocado and black olives.

Seafood Salad $10.50
A light and easy meal of prawns, crab, scallops and your favourite dressing. Ideally served with white wine.

Onion Soup with Beef and Cheese $2.65
Our own version of French onion soup topped with a generous sprinkling of grated parmesan.

Fishmonger's Special $2.95
Clam chowder served light yet creamy with the added piquancy of white wine.

Main Courses

Gratin of Fish of the Day with Sauces $9.55
Fillets gently broiled and served with a combination of béchamel and fresh tomato sauce.

Trout of the Jura $11.50
Whole trout poached in a Jura Rosé. Ideally served with a fine red wine.

Prawns on a Golden Base $13.75
Green prawns sautéed in ginger, garlic and lemon juice served on a bed of pawpaw.

Scallops with Mushrooms $11.65
Sautéed in butter, garlic and parsley, served in a pair of coquille shells. Ideally served with the House white wine.

Lobster with Herb Butter $19.45
Whole lobster baked in butter and fresh herbs and served with a squeeze of lemon.

Desserts

Creme Caramel $5.00
Homemade caramel custard.

Mousse au Chocolat $5.00
The House chocolate mousse.

Profiteroles $6.00
Two puffed pastries, stuffed with Amy's ice-cream and topped with a warm chocolate sauce.

Drinks

Coffee $1.50
Espresso $2.00
Cappuccino $2.50
Hot Tea $2.00

The Microsoft Office 2007 suite of programs (Microsoft Word, Microsoft Excel, Microsoft PowerPoint and Microsoft Access) all share the same drawing tools. This chapter will cover those tools. If you will not be using any of the Microsoft Office 2007 programs you can skip this module.

The Microsoft Office Drawing Tools are accessed from the Illustrations group of the Insert tab in the ribbon at the top of the Microsoft Office screen.

The next exercises will take you through the different types of tools that are available.

Drawing Shapes

The Drawing Shapes are accessed by clicking on the Shapes icon in the Insert group of the Ribbon (Toolbar).

You can select from a variety of different lines, basic shapes (such as circles, rectangles or common shapes), block arrows, flow chart symbols, callouts, and stars and banners.

Each object is created by dragging the mouse across the screen with the mouse button held down. Each shape drawn is said to be an object and these objects can be moved, copied, resized and deleted.

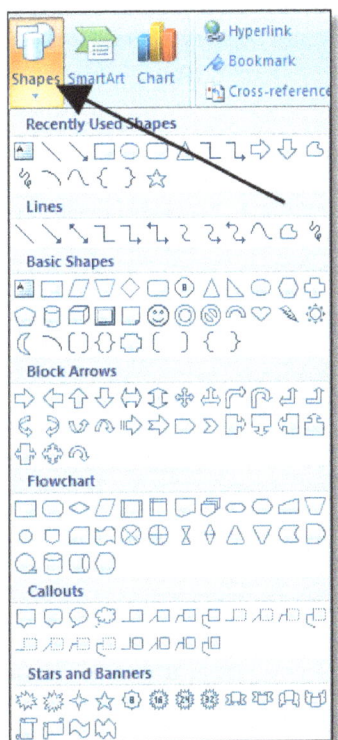

 **Drawing tools** exercise 1

Drawing Shapes

1. Try selecting the Rectangle tool from the Basic Shapes section of the Shapes palette and drag a rectangle anywhere on the screen.
2. Select the Rectangle tool from the Insert Shapes group of the Ribbon and try drawing another rectangle with the Shift key held down. You should only be able to create squares. The Shift key is called the constraint key because it forces objects to be perfect shapes.
3. Try drawing some lines, arrows and ovals. Try each of these with the shift key held down. For example:

Skills practised:

Drawing objects

Resizing objects

Moving objects

Copying objects

Deleting objects

Editing objects

Objects can be resized, moved, copied (duplicated) and deleted.

Drawing tools exercise 2

Skills practised:

Drawing objects

Resizing objects

Moving objects

Copying objects

Deleting objects

Editing objects

1. Click on the rectangle and notice that the rectangle has handles (small solid bars) around it. These allow the rectangle to be resized. The handles at the corners allow for diagonal resizing. The handles at the centre of the lines allow for either vertical or horizontal resizing and the green handle allows the object to be rotated.

2. Move the pointer over the bottom right corner handle until the pointer changes to a diagonal line with arrows at each end. Hold down the mouse button and drag the corner 'handle' towards the centre of the rectangle. This reduces the rectangle's size. Dragging in the other direction would have increased its size.

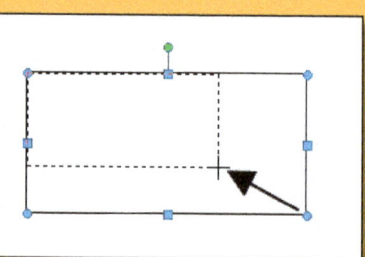

Deleting objects

1. You should have a number of objects on the screen at the moment.

2. Click the mouse button with the pointer over the border of an object to display its 'handles'. If an object is filled you can click on the centre of it to select it.

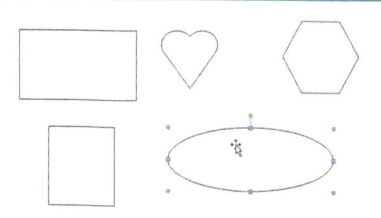

3. Press the backspace (or delete) key and the object will be removed.

4. Selecting Undo Clear from the Quick Access Toolbar at the top left of the screen (or press Ctrl+Z) will return a deleted object so long as nothing else has been entered, deleted or copied in the meantime. Try it.

Copying objects

1. Click on the Rectangle's border to display its handles, or redraw a rectangle if you do not have one on your screen.
2. Select Copy from the Clipboard group of the Home tab to send the rectangle to the clipboard (Ctrl+C or ⌘+C can also be pressed).
3. Select Paste from the Clipboard group of the Home tab (or press Ctrl+V or ⌘V) and a copy of the rectangle should be placed on the screen.

   Note: Cut works the same way as Copy except that the original Object is removed from the screen. An Object can be pasted as many times as required.

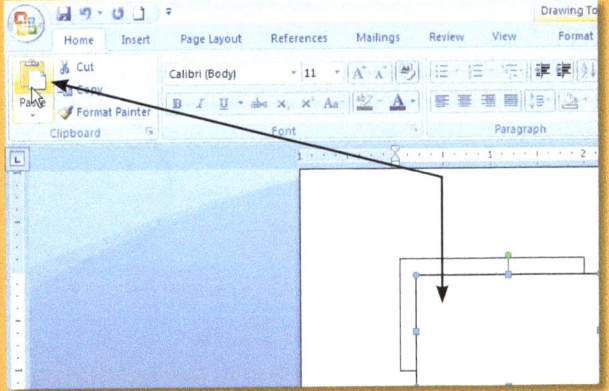

Moving objects

1. Move the pointer over the border of the rectangle (not near a handle). The pointer should have a cross-hair with arrows next to it indicating that it can be moved in any direction. Hold the mouse button down and drag the pasted rectangle to another part of the screen.
2. When moving objects the pointer must not be positioned over a 'handle'.

   Note: The Arrow keys can be used to nudge objects into place.
3. Try creating the following sketch of an old-fashioned TV set and edit it so that its lines are flush, that is, meet perfectly with one another.

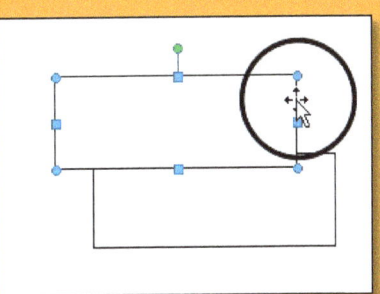

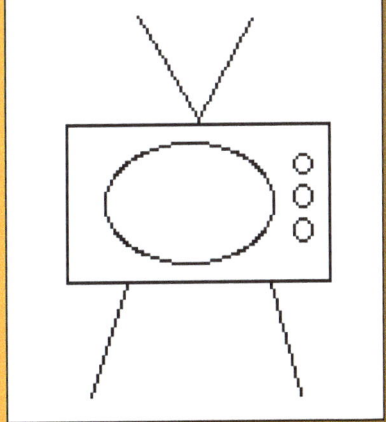

MODULE 3

Enhancing shapes

The appearance of shapes can be enhanced through the adding of shape fills, shape outlines, shadow effects and 3-D effects.

Drawing tools exercise 3

Skills practised:

Filling shapes

Adjusting borders

Adding shadows

3-D effects

Shape fills

1. Start a new Word document.
2. Open the Insert tab, select a shape, such as the Plaque shape, and drag a rectangle on a blank screen. The rectangle should take the plaque shape. All shapes are created this way.

3. Click on the Shape Fill icon in the ribbon and select a theme colour to fill the shape.

4. Click on the Shape Fill icon again in the ribbon, highlight Texture and select a texture to fill the shape with a pattern.

5. Click on the Shape Fill icon again in the ribbon, highlight Gradient and select a light or dark gradient to fill the shape with a gradient.

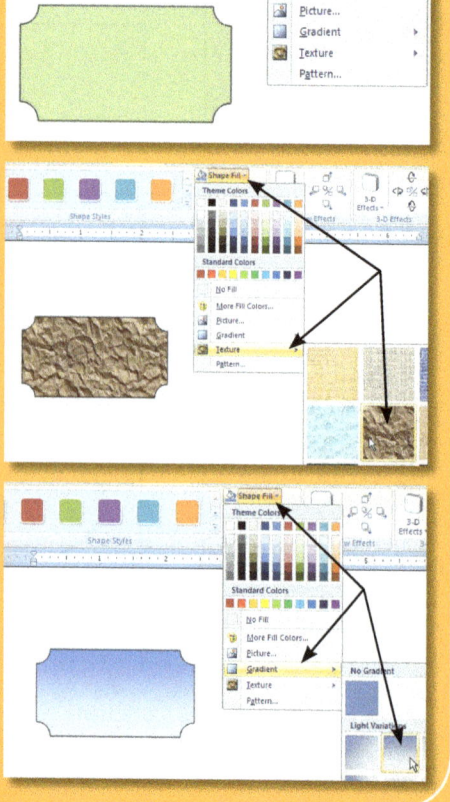

microsoft office drawing tools

84

Drawing tools exercise 4

Shape outline

1. Click on the Shape Outline icon in the ribbon, highlight Weight and select a thickness to change the thickness of the border around the shape.

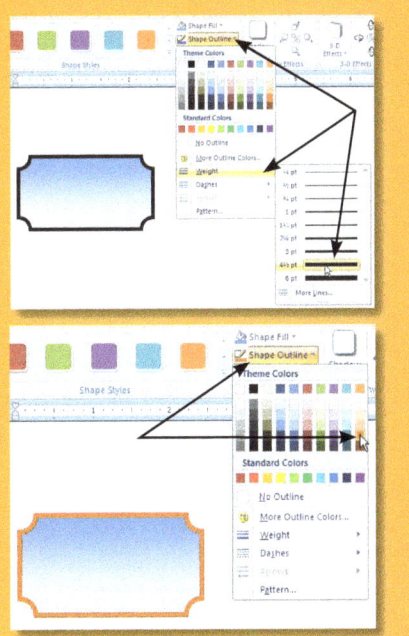

2. Click on the Shape Outline icon again in the ribbon, and select a theme colour to change the colour of the border around the shape.

   Note: You might like to also change the border to dashes or a pattern.

Drawing tools exercise 5

Shadow effects

1. Click on the Shadow Effects icon in the ribbon and select a Shadow Type to add a shadow to the shape.

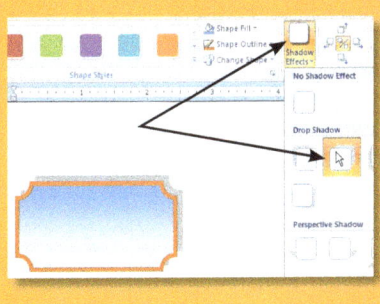

2. Use the Nudge shadow Arrows in the shadow Effects group of the ribbon to nudge the shadow so that it is larger or smaller.

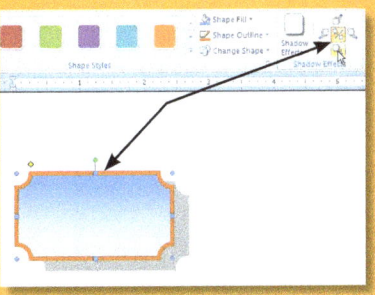

Drawing tools exercise 6

3-D Effects

1. Click on the 3-D Effects icon in the ribbon and select a 3-D Type to convert the shape into a three dimensional object.

2. Use the Tilt Arrows in the Shadow Effects group of the ribbon to rotate the 3-D object.

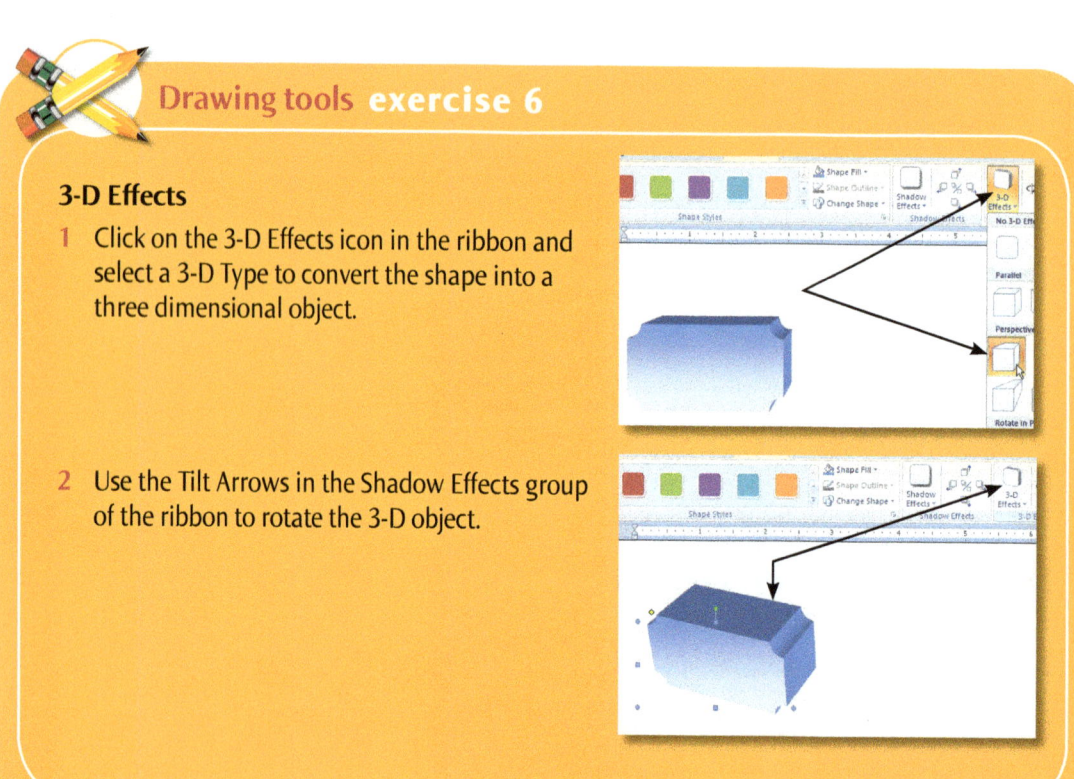

The Text Box tool

Text can be entered within some shapes, but you can also add a Text Box over a shape to add text to that shape. The Text Box tool is used to place text in a frame anywhere on the screen. It can be edited in the same way as the previous objects and the text in the Text Box can be formatted like any other text in Microsoft Office applications.

Drawing tools exercise 7

The Text Box tool

1. Select the Text Box shape in the Insert Shapes group of the ribbon and drag a frame within the plaque shape.

Skills practised:

The Text Box tool

Formatting text

Filling objects

Sent to back

Bring to front

Grouping objects

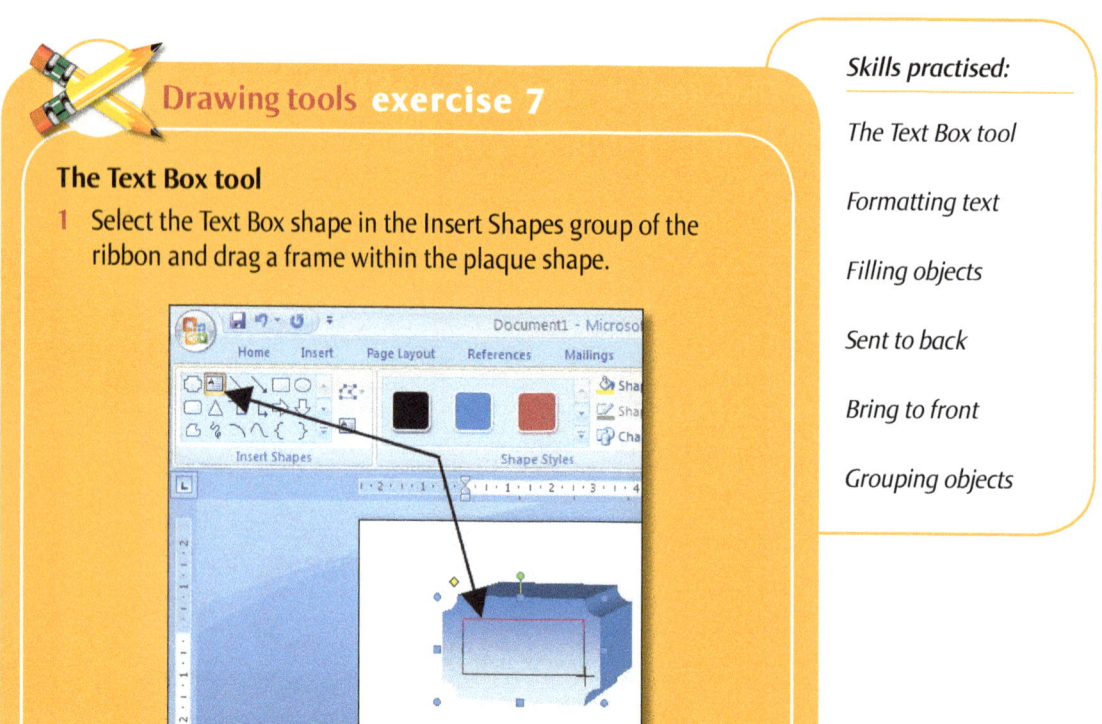

2. Enter your first name, then highlight the name and move the mouse pointer over the top border of the Text Box until the Mini Toolbar is displayed.

3. Set the text to a font of your choice, the size to 14 point, the style to bold, the alignment to centre and the font colour to a colour of your choice.

4. Click on the border of the Text Box, click on the Shape Fill icon in the ribbon and select No Fill to remove the white background from the Text Box.

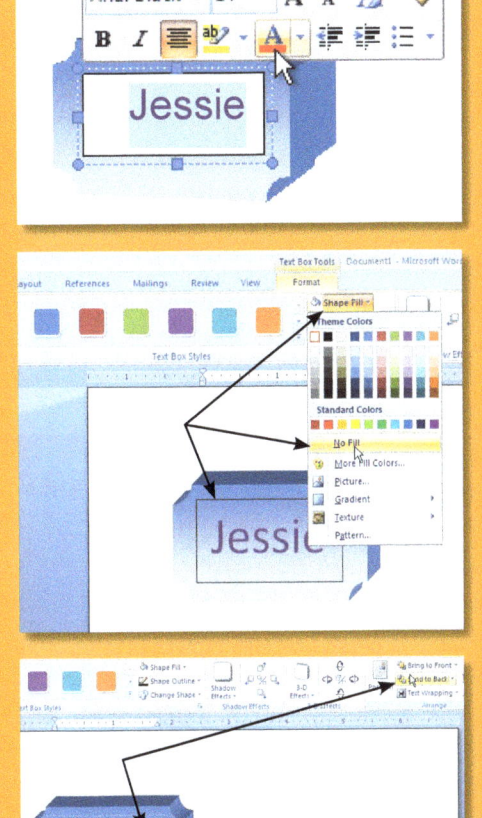

5. Click on Send to Back in the Arrange group of the ribbon to set the Text Box behind the plaque.

6. Click on Bring to Front in the Arrange group of the ribbon to return the Text Box to be on top of the plaque.

7. Hold down the Shift key and click on the plaque so that both it and the Text Box are selected, then click on the Group icon in the Arrange group of the ribbon and select Group to combine the two objects into one.

8. Try moving the objects to another part of the document. They both move together.

Note: Objects can be ungrouped by clicking on the Group icon in the Arrange group of the ribbon and selecting Ungroup.

Using Clip Art

Microsoft Office has its own library of graphics, called Clip Art, which can be inserted into documents when required. The graphics can include sketches, photographs or video clips. You can also insert graphics created in other programs such as Adobe Photoshop, Adobe Illustrator, Abobe FireWorks or PaintShop Pro.

Drawing tools exercise 8

Using Clip Art

1. Start a new Word document.
2. Open the Insert tab and click on the Clip Art button in the Illustrations group.
3. You will be provided with a panel at the right of the screen. Enter an animal name, for example, rabbit, in the Search For box and select Go.

4. Highlight the image you wish to insert, click on the arrow to the right of the image and select Insert. The animal image will be added to the screen at the cursor position.

   Note: You can also simply click on the image if you wish to insert it.

5. Try some of the Picture Styles in the ribbon and the picture frame around the image will be adjusted.

6. Click on the Picture Shape icon in the ribbon and select a shape, for example, the oval shape. The image will be adjusted to the selected shape.

7. The picture border can be turned off. Click on the Picture Border icon in the ribbon and select No Outline.

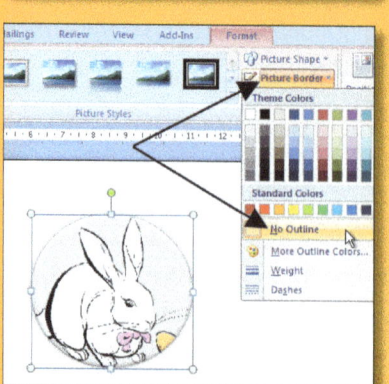

Skills practised:

Inserting Clip Art

Picture shapes

Picture styles

Picture borders

Picture effects

Brightness

Contrast

Recolour

8 Try some of the Picture Effects by clicking on the Picture Effects icon in the ribbon, highlighting the required effect and selecting a style. You can add shadows, reflections, glows, soft edges, bevels or 3-D rotation effects to Clip Art.

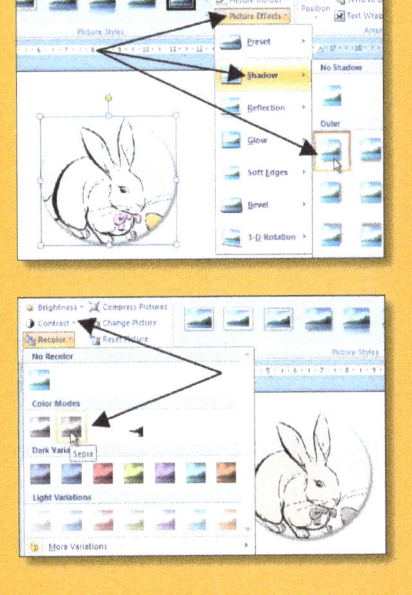

9 Try changing the Brightness, Contrast and Recolour of the image by selecting each in turn in the Adjust group of the ribbon. This allows you to adjust the colour and intensity of the Clip Art.

10 Try looking at some other Clip Art images.

Using WordArt

WordArt allows you to create fancy text headings.

Drawing tools exercise 9

Using WordArt

1 Start a new Microsoft Word document.

2 Click on the WordArt icon in the Text group of the Insert tab of the ribbon and select a WordArt style.

3 Enter your first name in the Edit WordArt Text frame, select OK and you will be returned to the Microsoft Word screen with the WordArt text displayed.

4 Click on the Edit Text icon in the Text group of the WordArt ribbon, and you will be returned to the Edit WordArt Text dialogue box. Try adding your last name just after your first name.

5 Select OK to complete the edit. You can increase the size of the WordArt by dragging a 'handle'.

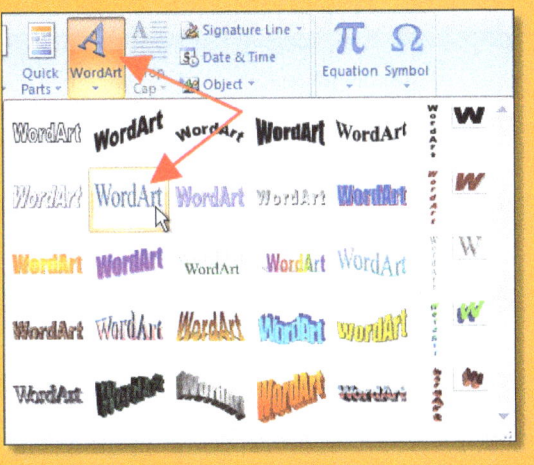

WordArt enhancements

WordArt offers you many options to adjust the appearance of your text. For example, you can change the WordArt shape, rotate the text, or change the colour of the text.

Drawing Tools exercise 10

Skills practised:

Inserting WordArt

Editing WordArt

Change shape

Shape fill

Shape outline

WordArt styles

1. Click on the Change Shape icon in the ribbon and select a shape to add a style to the WordArt text.

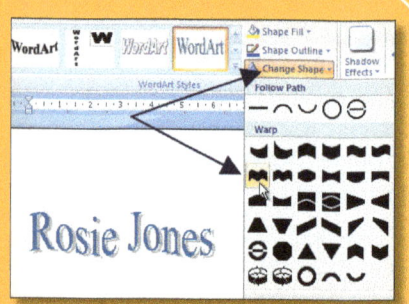

2. The Shape Fill icon allows you to change the fill colour or pattern of the WordArt text and the Shape Outline icon allows you to change the border of the wordArt.

3. The Position and Text Wrapping icons in the Arrange group of the ribbon allows you to control how normal text flows around the WordArt text.

4. The style of the WordArt text can be changed at any time. Select one of the WordArt styles in the WordArt Styles group in the ribbon and the text will be adjusted.

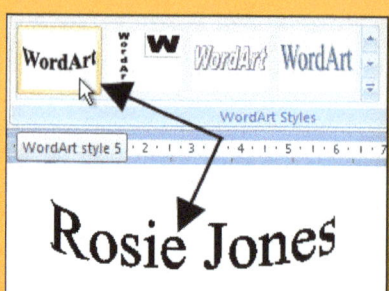

5. The Shadow Effects and 3-D Effects groups can be used to adjust the WordArt text in the same way as you did for shapes.

6. The Text group of the ribbon can be used to adjust the letter spacing, even the height of the letters, set the text to vertical or adjust the alignment of the text. Try each button in turn.

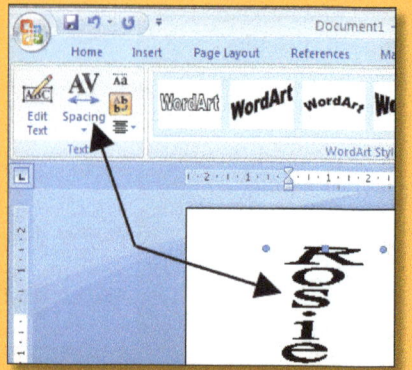

SmartArt Graphics

SmartArt Graphics allows you to insert predrawn diagrams such as organisation charts, relationship diagrams, pyramid charts and the like.

Drawing Tools exercise 11

Skills practised:

Inserting SmartArt

Entering text

Changing colours

Formatting boxes

Formatting text

SmartArt Graphics

1. Start a new Microsoft Word document.
2. Click on the SmartArt icon in the Insert tab of the ribbon, select Hierarchy and select the first Hierarchy SmartArt style.
3. Select OK and the Hierarchy chart will be added to the page.

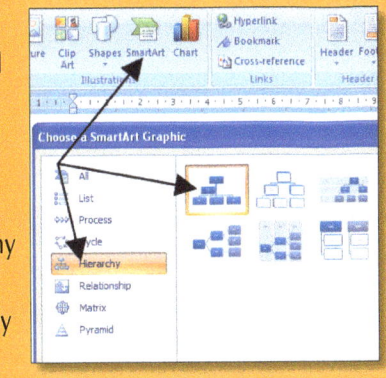

4. Click in the top box and enter Warrambool Sports Club, then enter Football, Netball and Cricket in the bottom three boxes.

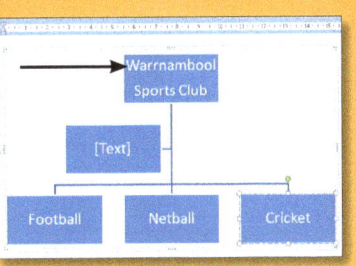

5. Click on the border of the box on the second row to select it then press the Delete or Backspace key to remove it from the chart.

6. A different colour scheme can be applied to the chart. Click on the Change Colors icon in the ribbon and select a different colour scheme for the chart.

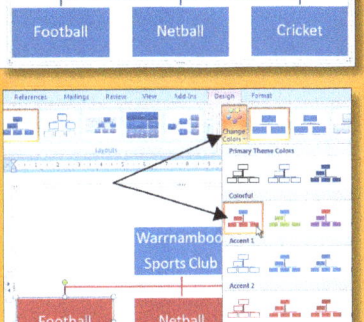

7. Individual boxes in the chart can be formatted. Select the top chart box, open the Format tab in the ribbon and apply a Shape Fill, a Shape Outline and a Shape Effect.

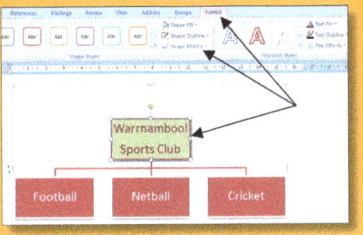

8 The text within the box can be formatted. Highlight Warrnambool Sports Club, then move the mouse pointer over the top of the box and the Mini Toolbar should be displayed.

9 Set the font to a font of your choice, the size to a larger size, the alignment to centre and select a font colour.

Note: You can also click on the Home tab in the ribbon to format the text.

10 Experiment with some other SmartArt charts.

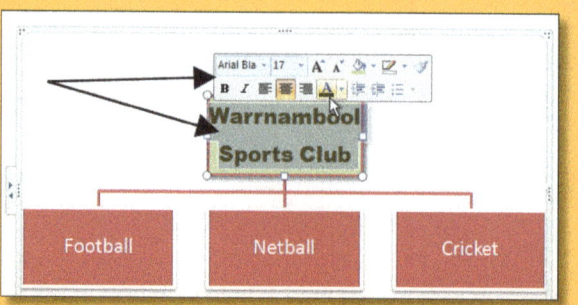

Aligning objects

When you enter multiple shapes into a document you can align those shapes accurately.

Drawing Tools exercise 12

Aligning objects

1 Start a new Microsoft Word document.
2 Draw three different rectangles on the page then hold down the Shift key and click on each rectangle so that each has its selection handles displayed.

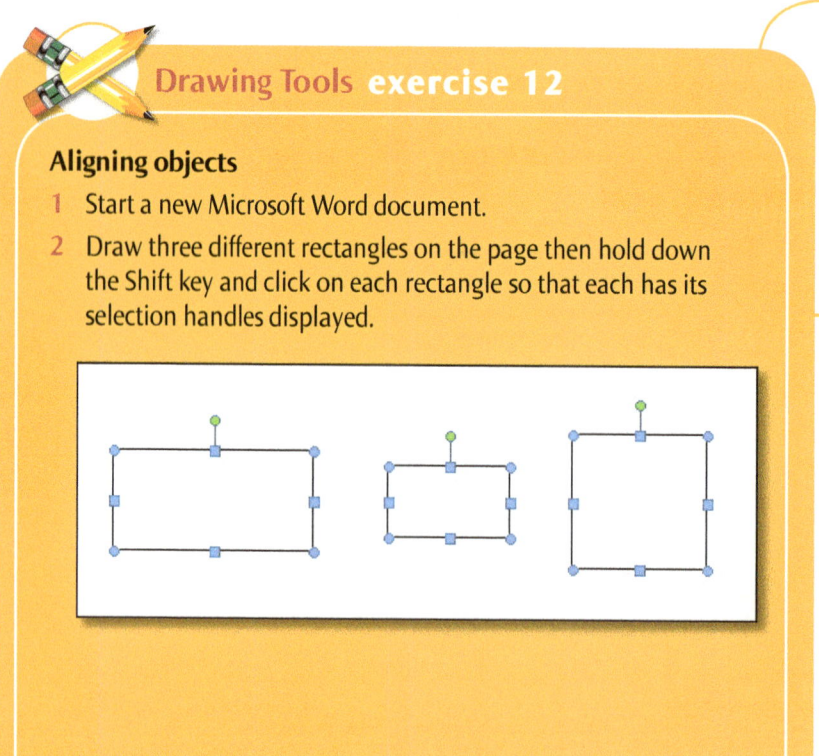

Skills practised:

Aligning shapes

Aligning top edges

Distributing space

3 Click on the Align icon in the Arrange group of the ribbon and select Align Top. The rectangles will be moved so that their top edges are level with one another.

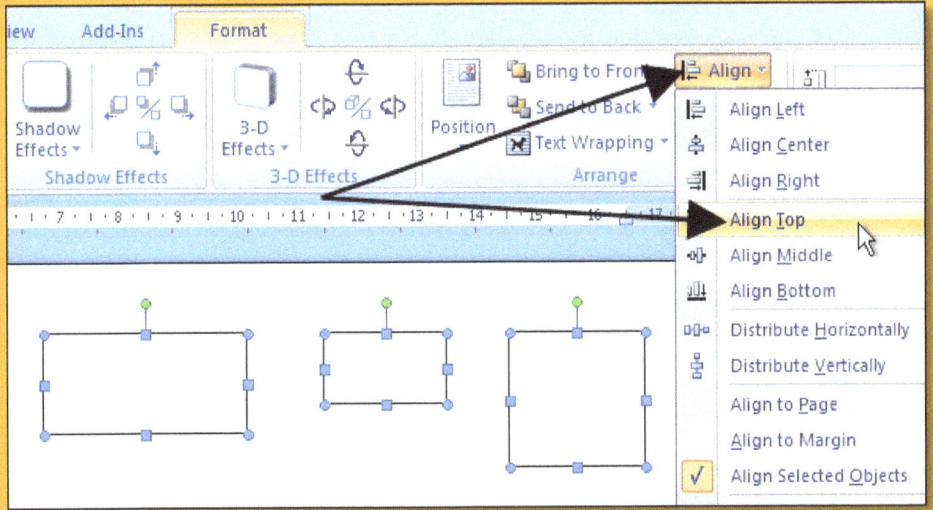

4 Click on the Align icon again in the ribbon and select Distribute Horizontally. This time the rectangles are moved so that the space between them is equal.

5 Experiment with some other alignments.

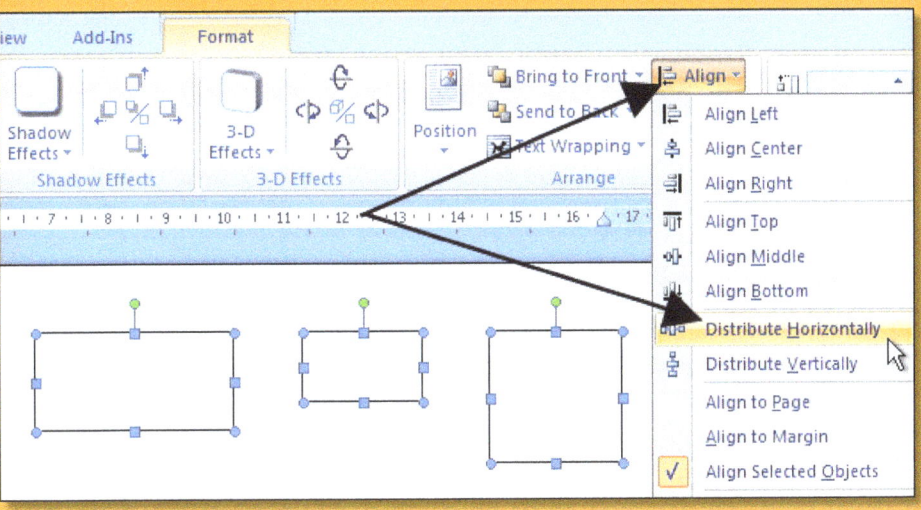

Drawing tools project

Safety in the Science room

Your Science teacher has decided to place safety posters around the Science room to hopefully help prevent accidents. Your teacher has asked you to produce one of the posters. You will need to find out four or five rules that are used to ensure safety in the Science room (such as always wear safety goggles when heating chemicals, etc.).

Collecting the data

Find four or five safety rules that exist in the Science room and look through the Clip Art to locate two appropriate graphics that you can use in your poster.

Project

Design the solution

Draw a mock-up sketch on paper of the poster that you will be creating. Indicate what heading you are going to use, the page border, the fonts and font sizes, where the rules will be placed on the page, where the graphics will be placed, etc. There is an example of a mock-up sketch in Module 2: 'Word processing project' on page 75.

Produce the solution

Use the Drawing Tools to create the poster.

Evaluate the solution

1. Ask other people to look at your publication and to give you feedback on the quality and accuracy of your poster. Describe what was said and what changes you made to your poster because of it.
2. What are the advantages of having posters produced on a computer as opposed to doing them manually? Are there any disadvantages?

Getting started

It is easy enough to record movie files these days on digital camcorders, cameras or mobile phones.

Movies can be made by combining several video files together, or simply using a collection of photos, or a combination of both. Sound tracks can be added as well as transition effects between movies and photos. You can also use Windows Movie Maker to edit clips, deleting sections as well as splitting clips.

In this module you will learn the basic skills to make a movie. There is lots more you can do with a movie but this will get you started.

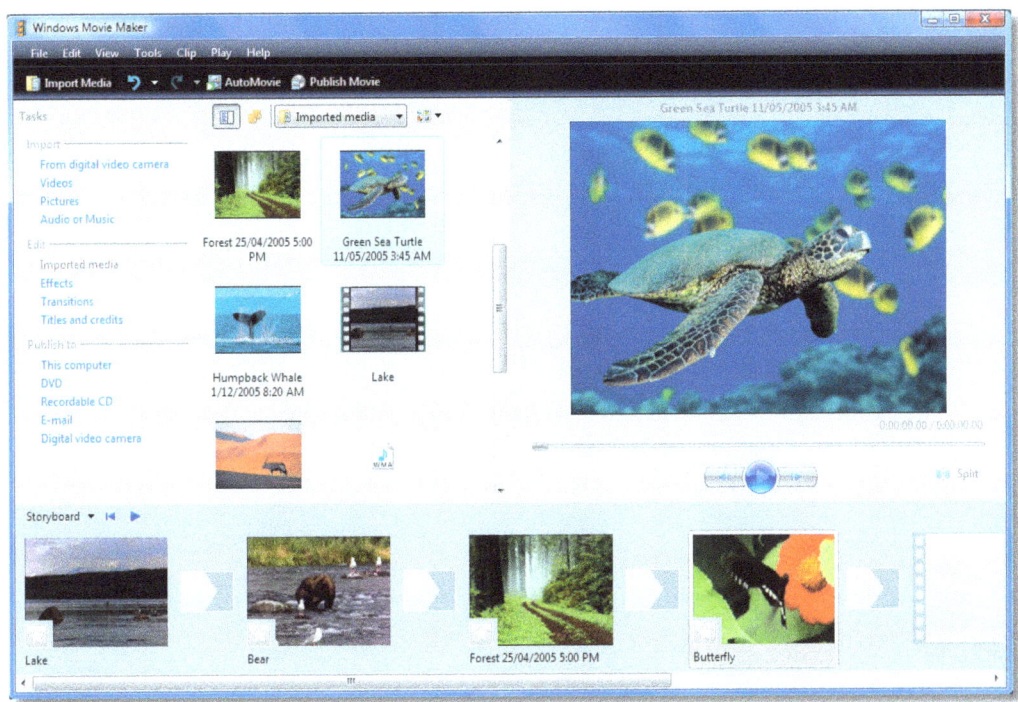

Making movies exercise 1

Start a movie project: Import movie files

1. Start Windows Movie Maker.
2. Click on **File** then **New Project** in the Menu bar.
3. Click on **File** then **Save Project** in the Menu bar.
4. Check with your teacher where to save this file as movie files are quite large and you may not be able to store them in your usual folder. **Save** the project with the name **My first movie** plus your initials (e.g. My first movie JD).

   The first step in your project is to import files to use. These files may be video, photos or audio.
5. Click on **Videos** in the **Import sections** on the Task pane. If you cannot see the Tasks pane click on **View** then **Tasks** in the menu bar until you can see it to the left of the window.

6. Locate the movies you want to import. The examples below are supplied with Windows Vista. Click on the first movie file, then hold down the **Ctrl** key and click on any other files you want to import. Click on the **Import** button.

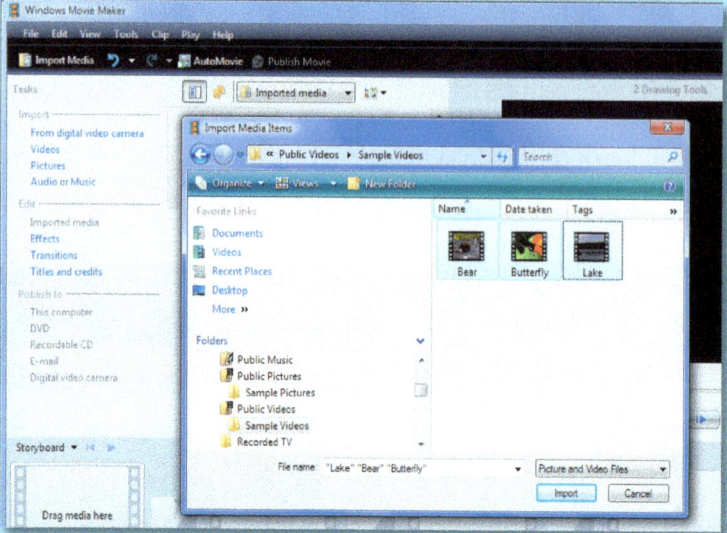

7. To play an imported clip, simply click on it and click on the **Play** button in the **Preview** pane.

8. You can also play the movie clip frame by frame by repeatedly clicking on the **Next Frame** and **Previous Frame** button.

Making movies exercise 2

Add clips to the Storyboard

1. Drag the clip down to the start of **Storyboard** area.
2. Drag others down if you have them in the order you want them to play.
3. Click the **Play** button in the **Preview** pane to check the clips and watch them all play in the order you have placed them.

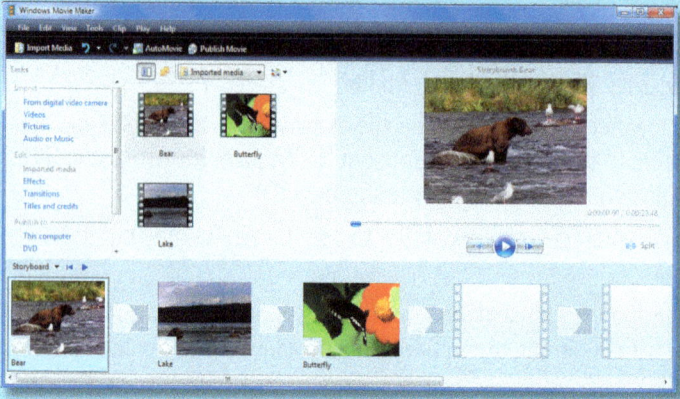

Making movies exercise 3

Add transitions

You can add a transition between each clip. The transitions are placed in the smaller blocks on the Storyboard between each clip.

1. Click on the **Location** droplist button and click on **Transitions**
2. Drag a transition down to each of the small placeholders on the **Storyboard**.
3. Click on the first clip on the Storyboard then click on the **Play** button in the **Preview** pane to view the effects of the transitions.

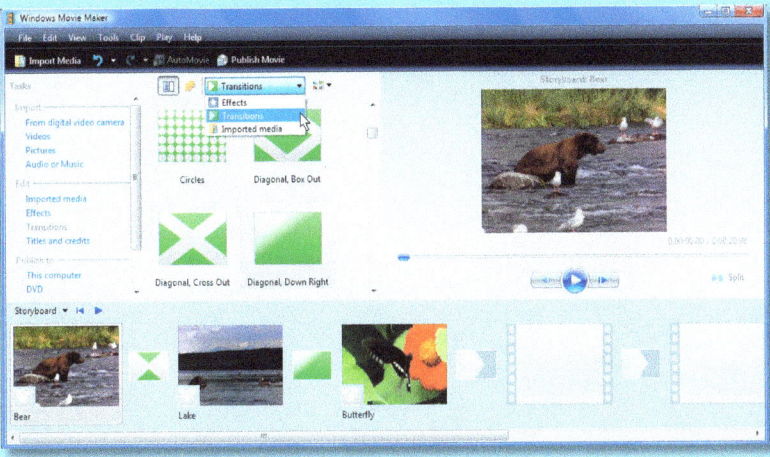

Motion and video effects

Motion and video effects are applied to a clip to modify how it appears when played. Below are some of the types of effects you can apply. Several effects can be applied to a clip, for example, you could use Sepia Tone, Film Age Old and Speed Up, Double to create a movie like an old silent film.

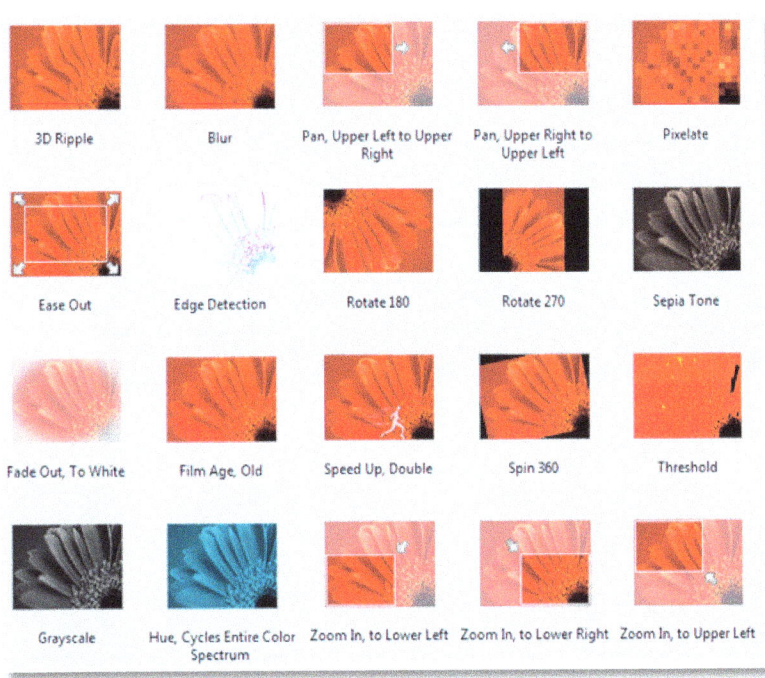

Making movies exercise 4

Add motion and video effects

1. Click on the **Location** droplist button and click on the **Effects** option so the various effects available to you are displayed.
2. Drag the effect you want to use down to the small star in the corner of each clip of the storyboard.

   The example below indicates an effect applied to the last clip.
3. Click on the **Play** button in the **Preview** pane to view the effect.

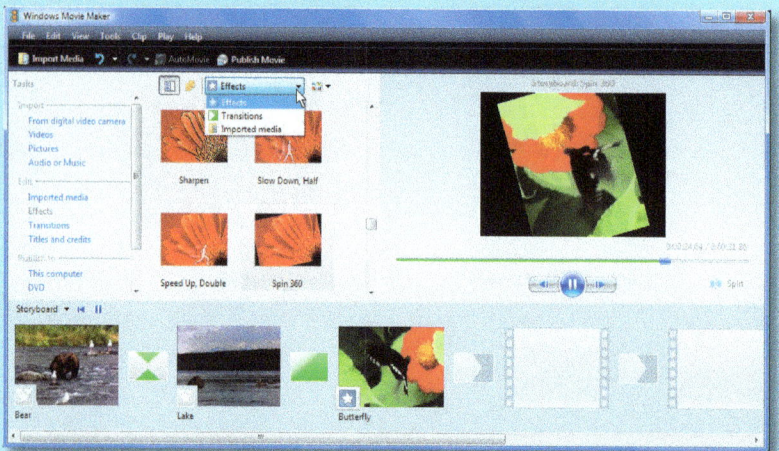

More than one effect can be applied to a clip. They can be removed again simply by clicking on the star and pressing the **Delete** key on the keyboard.

4. Apply an effect to each clip.

Making movies exercise 5

Adding titles to movie clips

Title slides can be inserted at the start of the movie, within it before a specific clip, over a clip and at the end of the movie.

1. Click on **Tools** then **Title and Credits** in the menu bar. Click on **Title at the beginning**.

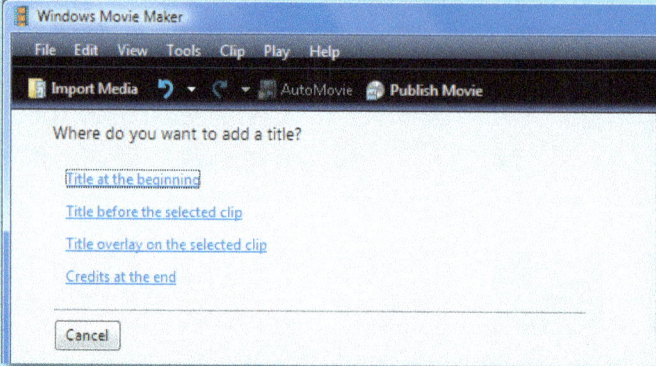

2. Click in the text box for the title and enter the text as you want it to appear.
3. Click on the **Change the title animation** link.

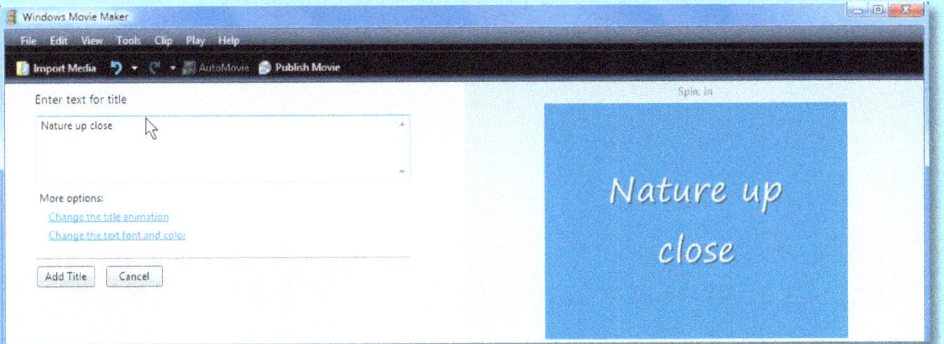

4. Scroll down the list box and click on various options, a preview of the animation will appear in the Preview pane. Click on the animation you want to use.

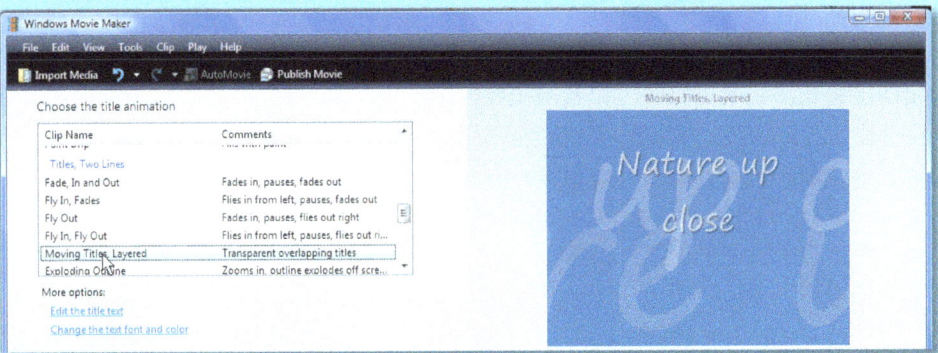

5. Click on **Change the text font and colour**. Click on the **Color** box to choose a different colour for the background.

6. Click on **Add Title** to complete the actions.

7 Repeat the process from steps 1 to 6 to add **Credits at the end**.

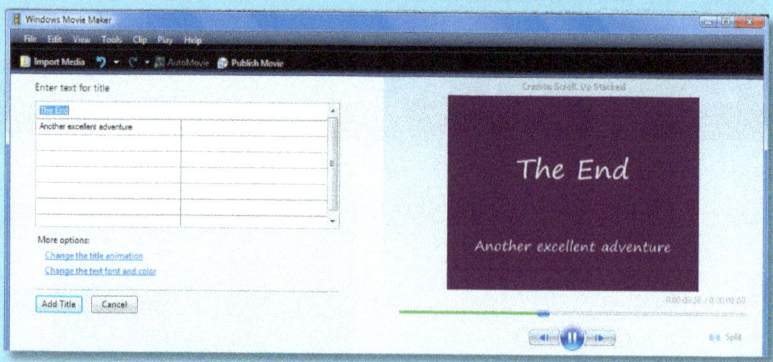

 **Making movies** exercise 6

Sound tracks

It is a very long time since the silent movies become talkies. It is very easy to add audio files to the movie. To do this you have to change from the Storyboard to the Timeline view.

1 Click on **View** then **Timeline** in the menu bar.
2 In the **Import** area click on **Audio** or **Music**. Locate the audio file you want to import. The example below is from the Sample Music folder that comes with Windows Vista. Click on the file and click on **Import**. The file will appear in the **Imported media** area.

Now to add the audio file to the movie.

3 Check that the green marker on the timeline is at the start of the clips – if it isn't, drag the marker in the **Preview** pane back to the start – this will move the timeline insertion point back to the start as well.
4 Drag the music down to the timeline and drop it at the start of the movie.

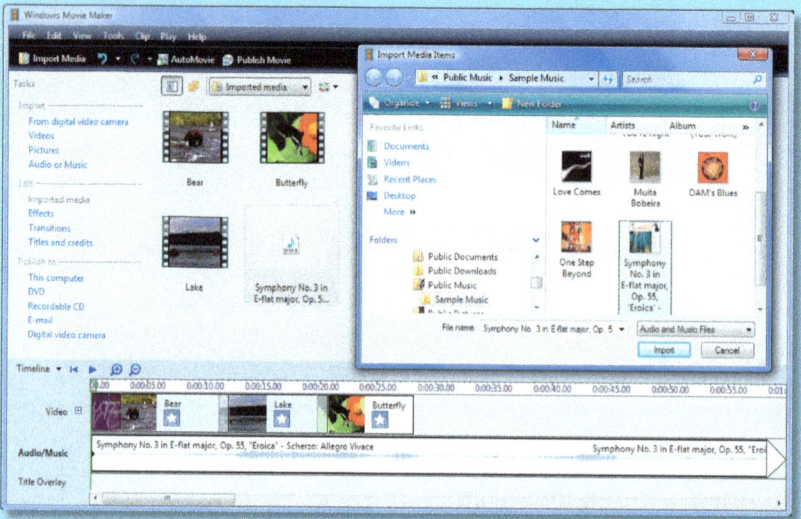

Notice that the audio file is a lot longer than the movie. It will have to be edited to shorten it.

Making movies exercise 7

Edit the movie

1. Click on the clip to be edited. It is encased in a border that is used to trim the video at either end.
2. Move the pointer over the right border of the first clip, when it changes, click, hold and drag in slowly, noting the frames in the preview pane so you can choose where to release the mouse and thus trim the clip to that point. As you drag, the remaining part of the clip is highlighted blue.

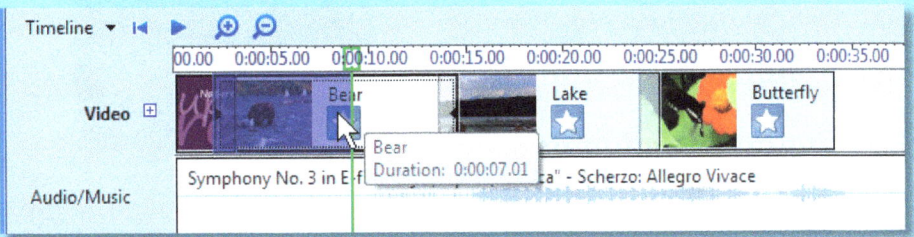

Once the mouse is the released the shorter clip is indicated and the other clips are automatically adjusted along the timeline.

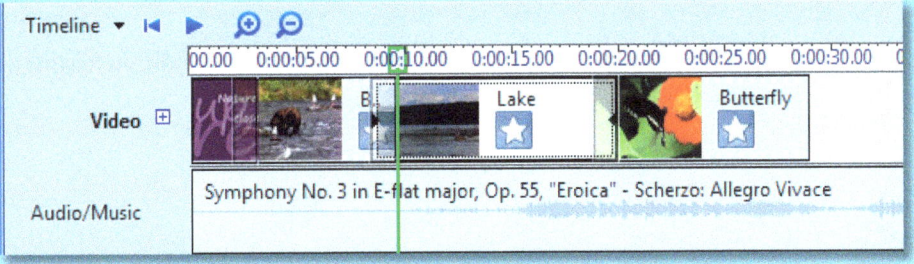

As music clips are often quite long it is easiest to use the scroll bar to find the end of the audio clip.

3. Use the scroll bar to scroll out to the end of the audio clip.
4. Click on it and repeat the process as for video clips, dragging back to the end of the combined video clips.

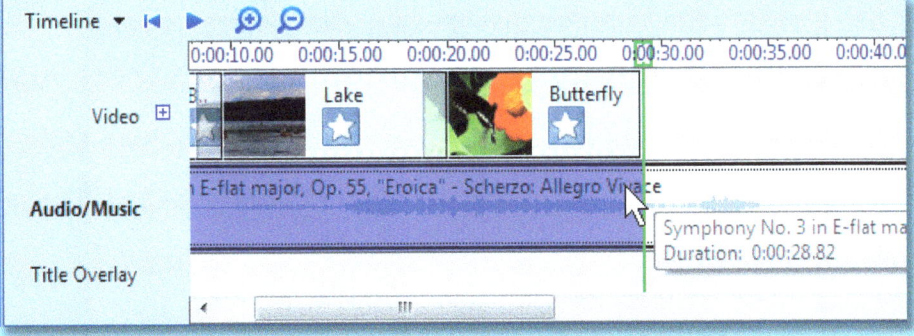

5. If you make a mistake you can use the **Undo** and **Redo** buttons to repair the damage.

6 You can also use the **Delete** key to delete any item from the Timeline or Storyboard. Now to check the transitions and effects.

7 Click on **View** then **Storyboard** in the menu bar to display it. From here you can make changes to the transitions and effects on each clip.

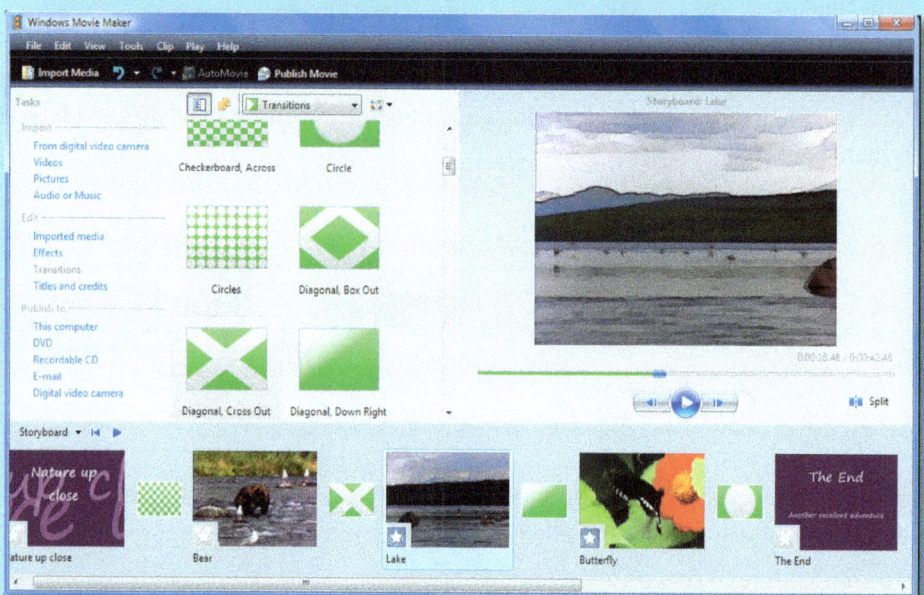

Note: If you want to edit a title or credit, click on it then click on **Edit** then **Edit Title** in the menu bar.

 Making movies exercise 8

Export movies

Once you have finished your movie, you want people to see it. You can use various formats to do this as explained in the Publish Movie dialogue box below.

1 Click on **File** then **Publish** to display the Publish Movie dialogue box.

2 Click on **This computer** if necessary then click on **Next**.

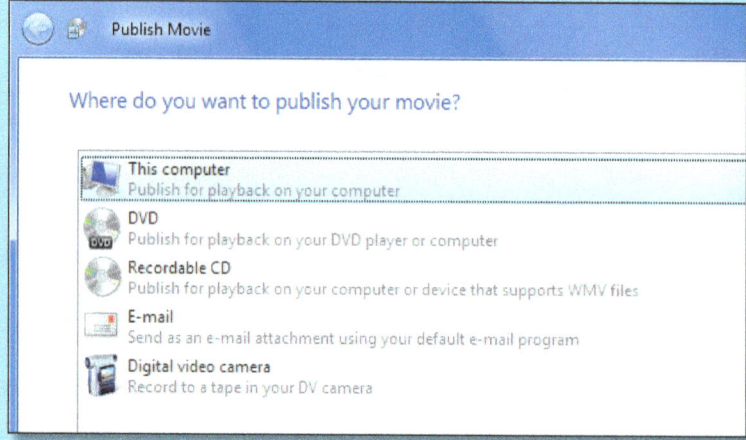

3 Enter a file name and a location then click on **Next**.
4 Leave setting on the default – **Best quality for playback on my computer**. Click on **Publish**.
5 Click on **Finish**.

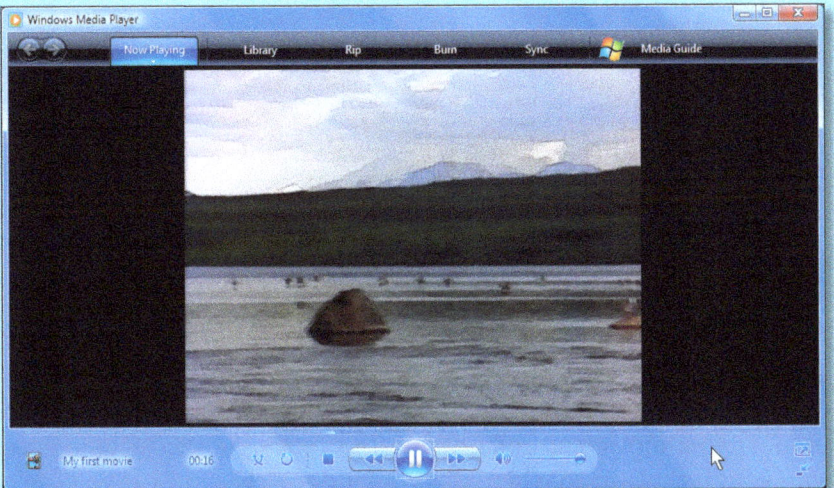

Windows Media Player will load and the movie will start to play.

6 When the movie has finished playing **Close** Windows Media Player.

 **Making movies** exercise 9

Preparing a DVD

1 Put a DVD in the DVD drive.
2 Click on **File** then **Publish** to display the Publish Movie dialogue box.
3 Click on **DVD** and **Next**. Click on **OK** to the prompt.

Windows Movie Maker will close the project and Windows DVD Maker will start.

4 Click on **Next** then click on **Burn** to create a basic DVD.

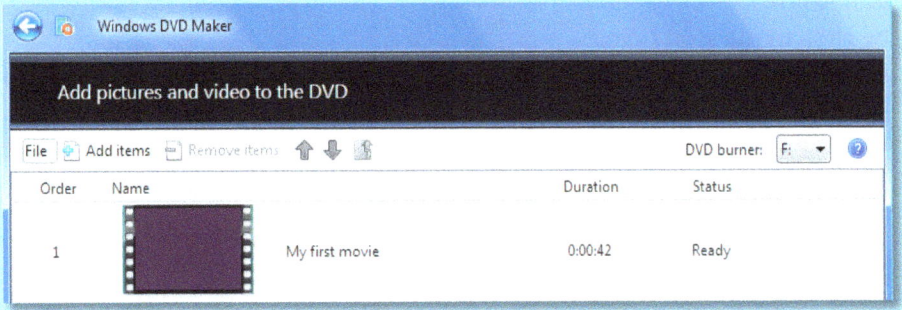

5 A prompt will appear when the DVD is complete, click on **Close**. Click on **Cancel** to close Windows DVD Maker and **No** to the prompt to save the project to Windows DVD Maker – it is still saved as a project in Windows Movie Maker.

Making movies exercise 10

Using Photos to make a movie

Return to the start of this module and work your way through again but this time using photos instead of movie clips. Make sure you apply motion and video effects to the photos.

Making movies project

Your task for this project is to create a movie based on a series of movie clips or photos about a particular theme. You can choose the theme or your teacher may set it.

Collecting the movie clips

Decide on a theme for your movie and collect five or six movie clips to include in your movie. Check with your teacher as to where you can find the clips or how you can create them if you have the appropriate equipment such as digital camcorder. Some possible topics might be:
- My favourite sports.
- A day at the zoo.
- A day at school.
- My favourite films.

Designing the movie

Draw sketches on paper to show how the movie clips will be joined together and indicate any text you are going to include.

Producing the movie

Produce the movie using Windows Movie Maker:
- Start a new project.
- Import the clips.
- Add the clips to the storyboard.
- Add titles to add the text.
- Apply transitions and special effects.
- Edit the movie as required.
- Add a sound track.

Export the movie

Export the movie to your computer. Check with your teach where to store it. Check the movie. If adjustments are required edit the movie project and export again.

MODULE 5

multimedia

What is multimedia?

Multi means many. **Media** is the type of material, for example:
- video (moving pictures)
- audio (sound)
- print (paper)
- graphics (pictures).

Multimedia is using more than one of the media types in a presentation. The most useful feature of multimedia is that the user has some control over when each type is used. For example, the user can choose to push a button to play some music or start a movie clip. If you have ever used a computer game or a program such as Microsoft Encarta you will have used multimedia. Multimedia is very popular in the education, information and entertainment fields.

Microsoft PowerPoint is commonly used to create multimedia files. We will assume you are using this program in this module.

PowerPoint produces slides that you can use for slide shows, overheads or handouts. Anytime you want to present information in an interesting way, PowerPoint is the program to use. PowerPoint is particularly useful because you can animate text and pictures to move around the slide, add sound for special effects and even videos.

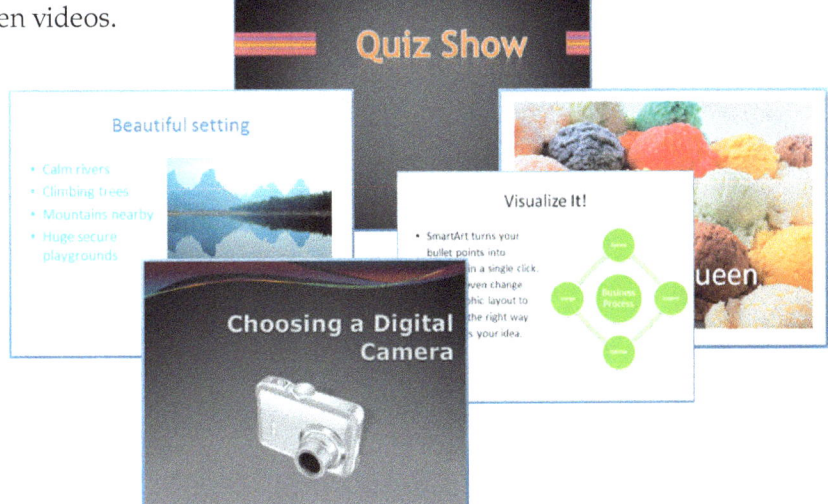

Creating a new presentation

To create a new presentation, follow the steps on the next page for Microsoft PowerPoint 2007.

Multimedia exercise 1

Creating a new presentation

1. Click on the **Office** button then **New**.
2. Click on **Blank Presentation** then **Create**.

    The Title Slide Layout is automatically used. You will see later how to apply a different layout.

    The slide layouts available are just various combinations of the objects available to PowerPoint.

    Some of the layouts are shown here. Content can be text, Clip Art, charts, graphics, SmartArt or other media clips.

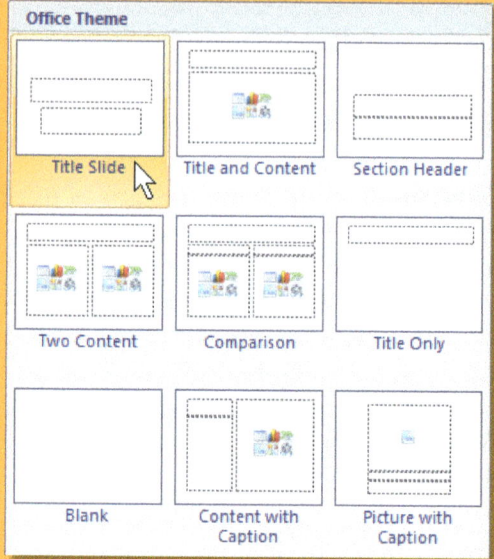

3. Type **Camp Summerhill** in the top place holder then **Kids Activities** in the lower placeholder, as shown to the right.

4. Click on the **Save** button, access your storage disk or folder, enter the name **Activities**, click on Save.
5. Click on the **New Slide** drop list arrow and click on the layout **Title and Content** – for the bulleted list layout – to add another slide after the first slide

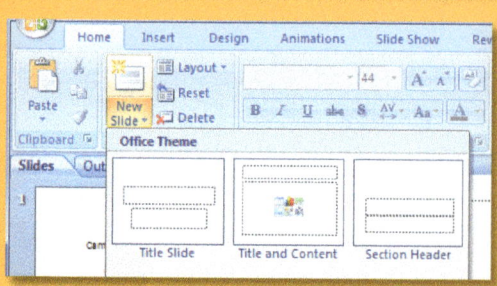

6. Enter the text below for **Slide No. 2**:

    Canoeing
    - Canoeing down calm rivers and streams

7. Repeat steps 5 to 6 to insert more new slides with the **Title and Content** layout entering the text as shown on the following page.

Slide No. 3
Insect studies
- Catch butterflies and other insects
- Study their form and features

Slide No. 4
Fishing

Slide No. 5
Gardening

Slide No. 6
Bowls

Slide No. 7
Football

Entering text

To enter text into your presentation, follow the steps below.

 Multimedia exercise 2

1. Create a new presentation.
2. Click on the **Save** button, access your storage disk or folder, enter the name **Facilities**, click on Save.
3. Enter the text as shown below for Slide No. 1.
4. Use the **New Slide** button to add new slides with the **Title and Content** layout and enter text onto each slide, as outlined below (this will be used later so make sure you enter all the text).

Slide No. 1
Camp Summerhill
Facilities

Slide No. 2
Beautiful setting
- Calm rivers
- Climbing trees
- Mountains nearby
- Huge secure playgrounds

Slide No. 3
Food
- Wide range of foods
- Vegetarian
- Special chef

Slide No. 4
Sleeping quarters
- Comfy beds
- Hot showers
- Private drawers and cupboards

Slide No. 5
Medical care
- Qualified doctor on call
- 24-hour nursing sister
- Fully-equipped nursing bay

Slide No. 6
Parent contact
- Telephone
- Daily mail service
- Sunday visits encouraged for family picnics

Slide No. 7
Sporting equipment
- Up-to-date equipment

Formatting text

Formatting text can emphasise particular points. Formatting of text in PowerPoint is much the same to other Microsoft programs. To format a single word you need only place the mouse within the word rather than highlight the whole word. If you want to format a whole line it still needs to be highlighted.

Multimedia exercise 3

Formatting text

1. Open the file **Activities** created in Exercise 1.
2. Highlight the slide title.
3. Click on the drop list arrow of the **Font** box.
4. Click on the desired font.
5. Click on the **Font Size** box and scroll to the desired size and click.
6. Experiment with other buttons on the **Home** ribbon shown below and format the headings as shown on the next page.

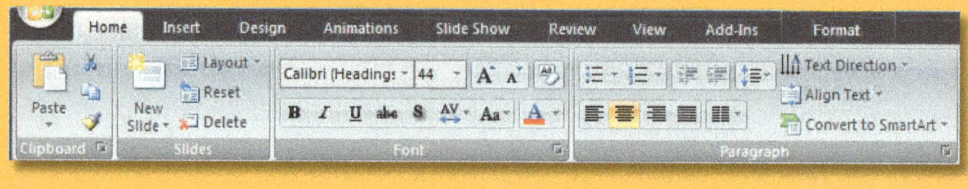

Inserting graphics

Clip Art can be inserted onto any slide (the slide does not have to have the specific Clip Art layout).

Multimedia exercise 4

Inserting graphics

1. Check that the file **Activities** (created in Exercise 1) is displayed.
2. Display the slide that is to have the Clip Art added.
3. Click on the tab **Insert** then **Clip Art** to display the Clip Art task pane.
4. Enter a search term in the **Search for** box then click on **Go** to display the possible choices.
5. Click on the piece of Clip Art you want to use. The Clip Art will be put onto the slide currently selected. The Clip Art will be in the middle of the slide.

6 Drag the Clip Art to an appropriate location and resize it if necessary.
7 Add a piece of Clip Art to each slide.
8 **Save** and **close** the file.

Starting from scratch

Now you can create another presentation with text and graphics.

 **Multimedia exercise 5**

Starting from scratch
1 Create a new blank file called **Cinemania**.
2 Add **New Slides** and enter the text shown on the next page.
3 Insert Clip Art into the slides – choose your own or use the following examples.
4 Format the text.
5 Change the layout and position of text and Clip Art.
6 Click on the **Slide Show** tab then **From the Beginning** to run the slide show – click the mouse to move from slide to slide.
7 **Save** and **close** the file.

MODULE 5

multimedia

Cinemania

To display this way call 9252 5454

Bella Dancing
- Get fit
- Stay fit
- Socialise
- All levels
- Classes
- Socials
- Mixed
- Crèche

The Soup Ladle

Delicious and nutritious

15 Market Lane
9234 5678

The Ice Queen

Multimedia exercise 6

More graphics

1. Open the file you created in exercise 2 called **Facilities**.
2. Insert graphics onto each slide to illustrate the points – be creative, you don't have to use exactly what is displayed here and on the following page.
3. **Save** and **close** the file.

Camp Summerhill

Facilities

Beautiful setting
- Calm rivers
- Climbing trees
- Mountains nearby
- Huge secure playgrounds

Food

- Wide range of foods
- Vegetarian
- Special Chef

Sleeping quarters
- Comfy beds
- Hot showers
- Private drawers and cupboards

Slide transitions

A slide transition is the way we move from one slide to the next in a slide show. For example, one slide may fade out to the sides as the next appears. PowerPoint has 53 varieties of transitions. The transition type can be set for a group of slides or just one. A transition speed and sound can also be set.

Multimedia exercise 7

Slide transitions

1. Open the file **Activities**.
2. Display the first slide.
3. Click on the **Animations** tab in the ribbon. Move the mouse over each of the transition effects for a preview of how the transition will look.

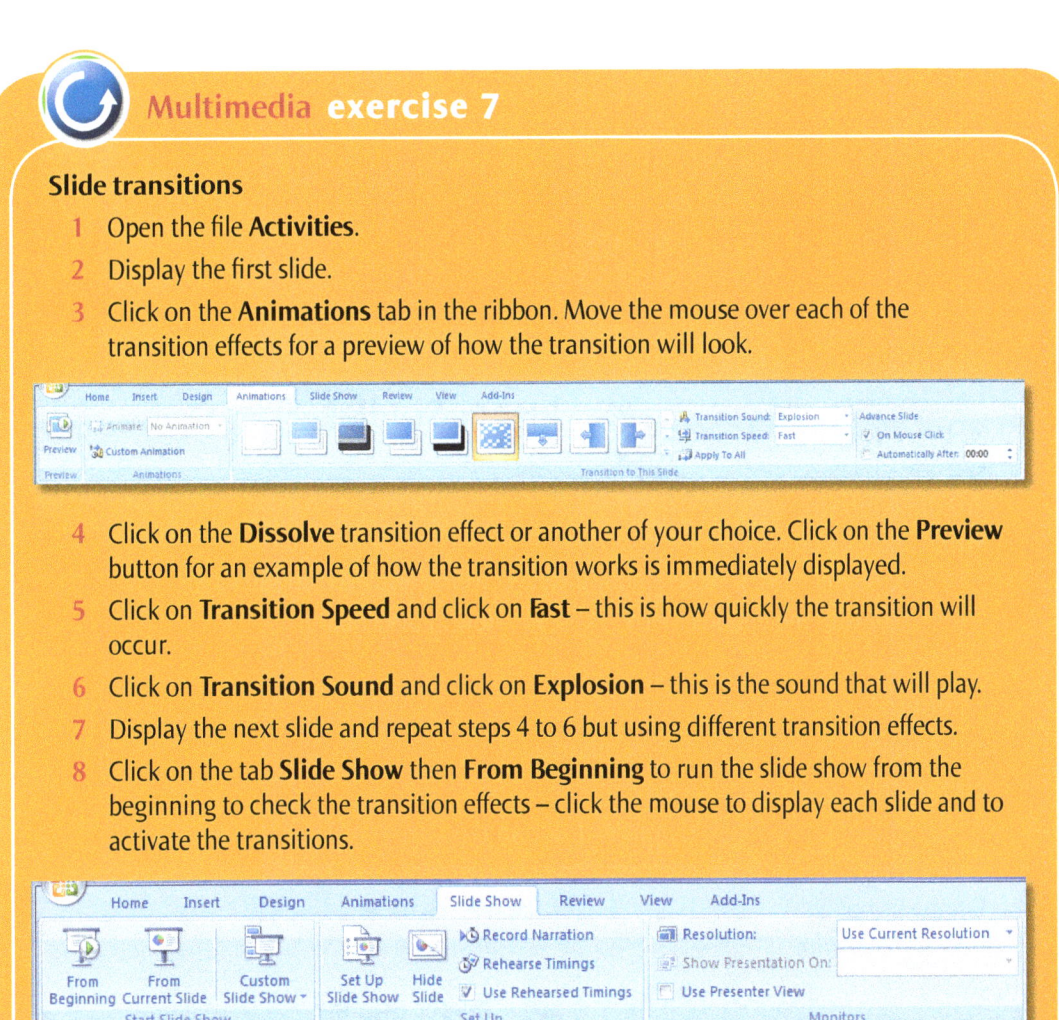

4. Click on the **Dissolve** transition effect or another of your choice. Click on the **Preview** button for an example of how the transition works is immediately displayed.
5. Click on **Transition Speed** and click on **Fast** – this is how quickly the transition will occur.
6. Click on **Transition Sound** and click on **Explosion** – this is the sound that will play.
7. Display the next slide and repeat steps 4 to 6 but using different transition effects.
8. Click on the tab **Slide Show** then **From Beginning** to run the slide show from the beginning to check the transition effects – click the mouse to display each slide and to activate the transitions.

9. **Save** and **close** the file.
10. Open other presentations you have created and apply slide transitions to them.

MODULE 5

Animating slides for a slide show

Animating a slide is when the text or Clip Art or other objects on the slide are activated to move around or change in some way. PowerPoint has many different animation effects.

Multimedia exercise 8

Animating slides for a slide show

1. Open the file called **Activities**.
2. Display the slide titled **Insect Studies**.
3. Click on the **Animations** tab and click on the **Custom Animation** button. This box enables us to choose which element is to be animated, in what order, and how.
4. Select the **Title placeholder**.
5. Click on the **Add Effect** button in the **Custom Animation** task pane. You have several choices on the method of appearance.
6. Click on **Entrance** and then **Fly in** from the list of options that appears.

7. Click on the drop list button for **Direction** and click on **From Left**. Click on the drop list button for **Speed** and click on **Very fast**. As you make your selections the effect will be displayed on the slide.

8. Experiment with the options then click on **Preview** in the ribbon.

Animating Clip Art objects

Other elements of the slide can also be automated.

1. Click on the Clip Art object to select it.
2. Click on **Add Effect** in the **Custom Animation** task pane.
3. Click on the **Emphasis** option then click on **Spin**.

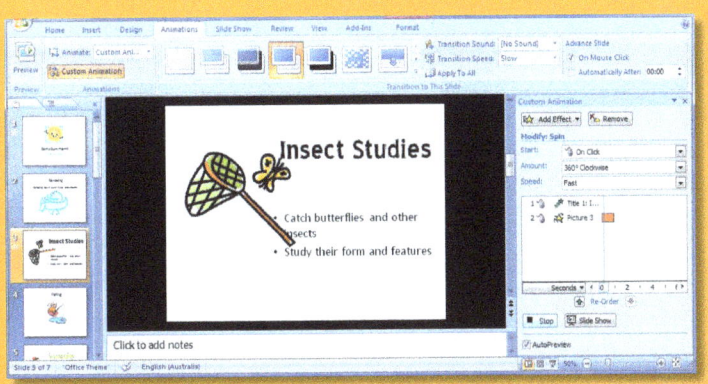

4 Click on the drop list button for **Amount** and select the amount of rotation.

5 Click on the drop list button for **Speed** and check how fast you want the object to move.

6 Experiment with the options then click on **Preview** or **Play**.

Building bullets

Bullets can be set to build one line at a time on the screen. This is particularly useful for adding impact to each point.

 Multimedia **exercise 9**

Building bullets

1 Click on placeholder for the bulleted list.
2 Click on the **Add Effects** button in the **Custom Animation** task pane.
4 Click on the **Entrance** option then the **Box** option.
5 Click on the **Preview** button to check the effect.

Notice that a 3 and 4 appear next to each point in the list even though you have only applied one effect. This indicates that when the slide show is run, each bullet will only appear on a click of the mouse by the user, thus the list of bullets is built on screen.

6 Apply custom animation to the other slides in the presentation.
7 **Save** and **close**.

Using masters

When you first start to use PowerPoint it is very easy to get carried away with all the great things you can do. The danger in this is that others looking at the slide show become distracted with all the changes and the message can be lost. The purpose of setting a master background is so that each slide has a standard look. When you create master slides, you incorporate formatting, drawing tools, graphics and automatic fields such as slide number or date.

In exercises 10 to 16 you will create a master for a school camp report. You will:

- apply a background
- insert a page number
- insert a footer along the bottom border that has the name of the school camp
- insert a Clip Art piece such as a tent in the top left corner.

Multimedia exercise 10

Using masters

There are three different Master Views: Slide Master, Handout Master and Notes Master.

1. Start a **New** presentation with a title **Slide layout**.
2. Click on the **View** tab then the **Slide Master** button.
3. Click on the first slide in the pane at the left.

   The slide will appear in Slide Master View as shown below. The Slide Master is divided into two distinct areas, the Master title placeholder and a Master text placeholder. The Master title and Master text control the way the title and text will appear on all your slides in slide view. For example, if you change the font to Arial and Italic for the title, this is the way the title text will initially be formatted on each slide.

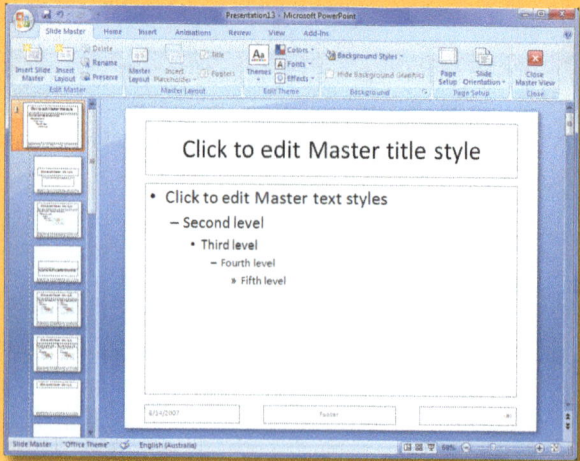

Formatting the master text

1. Highlight the text in the **Master title** placeholder.
2. Format it to be a different font style and size or use the **Fonts** button in the **Edit Theme** group on the ribbon.

Formatting master bullets

Bullets are used in text lists to emphasise items. The bullets currently used for this slide are displayed next to each level of text. PowerPoint has a huge range of bullets that can be selected from.

Multimedia exercise 11

Formatting masters

1. Click anywhere on the line that reads **Click to edit Master text styles**.
2. Click on the **Home** tab and click on the **Bullet** drop list button.
3. Click on **Bullets and Numbering** to display the **Bullets and Numbering** dialog box, as shown below, with the bullet currently in use highlighted among the set of available bullets. The size and colour of the bullet can also be adjusted here.
4. Click on the **Customize** button. The Symbol dialog box appears.
5. Click on the **Fonts** drop list button and click on a set – **Windings** is always good for a range of bullets.
6. Click on the bullet you want to use, then click **OK** and **OK** again. You will be returned to the **Master** view of the slide. The bullet you chose will be displayed.
7. Repeat the process to alter the other bullets.
8. Click on the **Master View** tab, then the **Close Master View** button to return to the Slide view.

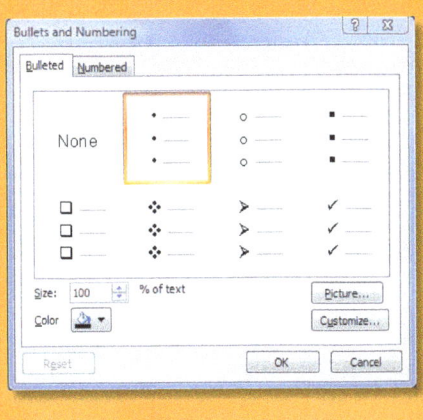

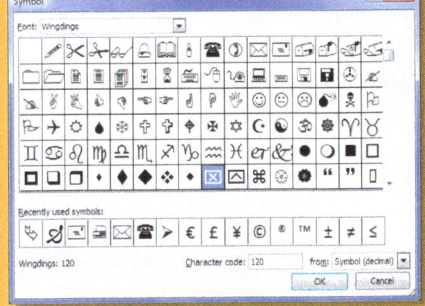

Adding background items

Background items appear on all slides. Background items are:

- date and time
- text footers
- slide numbers
- pictures
- shapes
- graphic watermarks.

You can insert a Footer, Date and Time and Slide numbers without being in Master View. However, you must be in Master view to format them to be the same on each slide.

Multimedia exercise 12

Adding background items

1. Click on the **Insert** tab then click on the **Header and Footer** button. The background items can be activated in the Header and Footer dialog box.

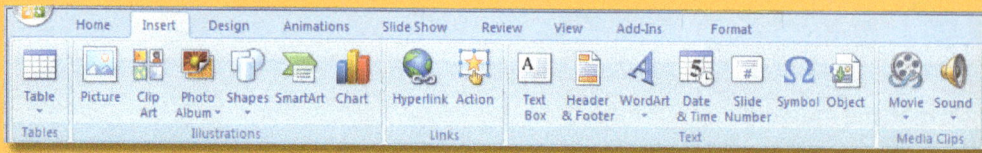

Adding a slide number

1. With the Header and Footer dialog box displayed, click into the **Slide number** check box.
2. Click on **Apply to All**.

Adding a footer

1. Click on the **Header and Footer** button again.
2. Click on the **Footer** option so a tick appears.
3. Type **Hilltop School Camps** or some text of your own in the **Footer** box.

Don't show background items on title slide

Often you do not want the background items to appear on the title slide.

1. Click on the **Don't show on title slide** so a tick appears.
2. Click on **Apply to All**.

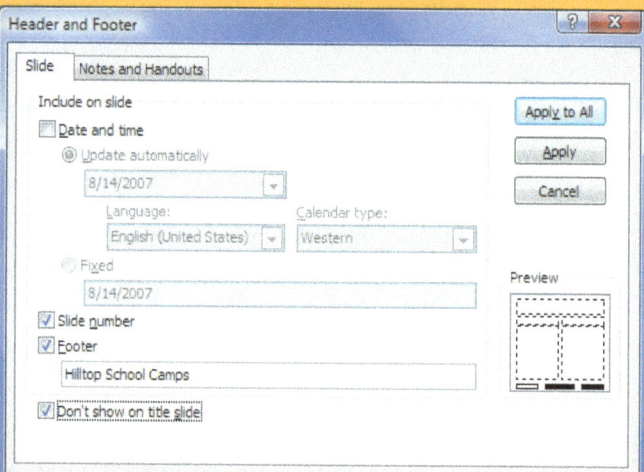

Adding the date and time

There is a choice with date and time of inserting a fixed date or inserting a date that is automatically updated to the current time. In the Master view:

1. Click on **Header and Footer** on the **Insert** tab in the ribbon.
2. Click into the **Date and time** check box so a tick appears.
3. Click on the **Fixed** option and enter a date in the box.

   Or if you want the date to update automatically:

4. Click on the **Update automatically** box and click on the drop list button to select the format for the date.
5. Click on **Apply to All**.

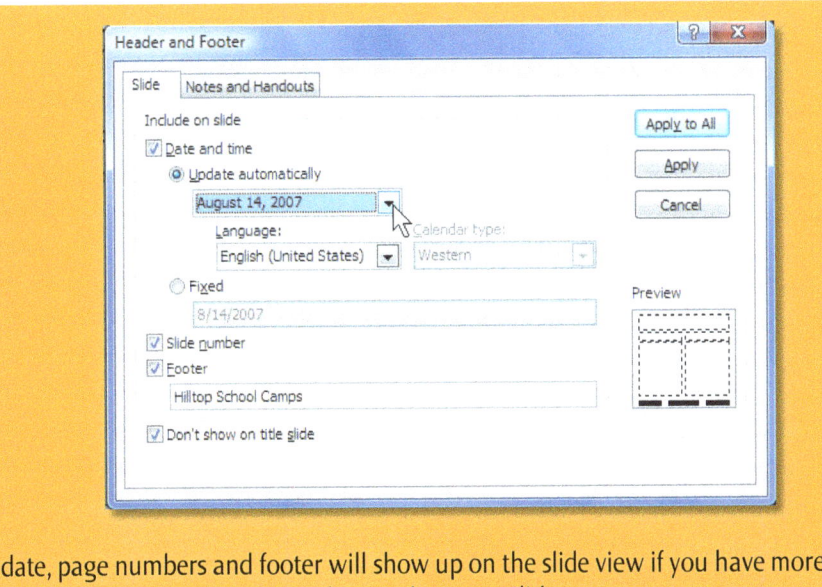

The date, page numbers and footer will show up on the slide view if you have more than one slide. Add another slide so you have at least two slides.

Adding a picture to a master

Any picture or logo can be put on the slide master to appear on each slide. This must be done in Master View.

 **Multimedia exercise 13**

Adding a picture to a master
1. Click on the **View** tab then the **Slide Master** in the ribbon. The slide will appear in Slide Master view. Click on the first slide in the pane to the left.
2. Click on the **Insert** tab then click on the **Clip Art** button.
3. Insert a piece of Clip Art that represents a camping or mountain scene.
4. The Clip Art will appear in the middle of the slide, so it will have to be moved. Resize and move the Clip Art and the title so they appear together at the top of the slide.

   Your Master should look something like this, depending on the choices you made.

5. Click on the **Close Master View** button to return to the Slide view. The features you added to the slide master will appear on the slides.

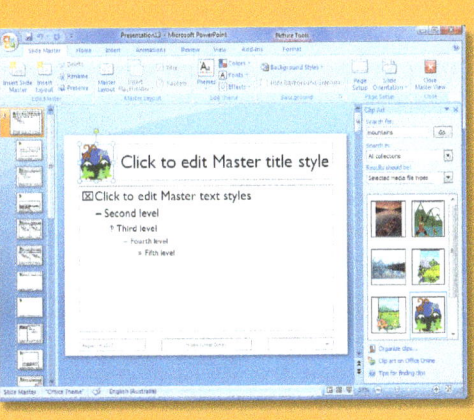

Following the master

In PowerPoint you have control of the master views. Each slide automatically follows the master (i.e. displays the elements you added to the master). You have the option of displaying the background items from the slide master on each type of slide layout in the presentation.

 Multimedia exercise 14

Following master background items

To omit background graphic items from the slide:

1. Click on the **View** tab and click on **Slide Master**.
2. Click on the **Section Header Layout** on the left, as highlighted.
3. Click on the **Footers** box so the tick is cleared and the **Hide Background Graphics** box so a tick appears. Neither of these master items is displayed when this type of slide layout is used.
4. Click on the **Close Master View** button.

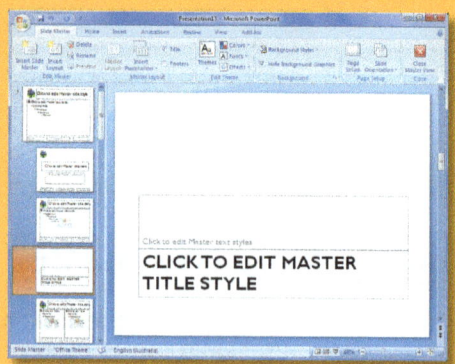

 Multimedia exercise 15

Apply and modify a theme design

A theme can be applied to your master.

1. Click on the **View** tab then click on **Slide Master**.
2. Click on the **Themes** drop list button in the ribbon and click on the theme you want to use. How the theme is applied to each type of Slide layout is displayed in the left hand pane.
3. Click on the **Colors** drop list button to display suggestions for sets of colours.
4. Click on a colour scheme that you like.
5. **Save** and **close** the file.

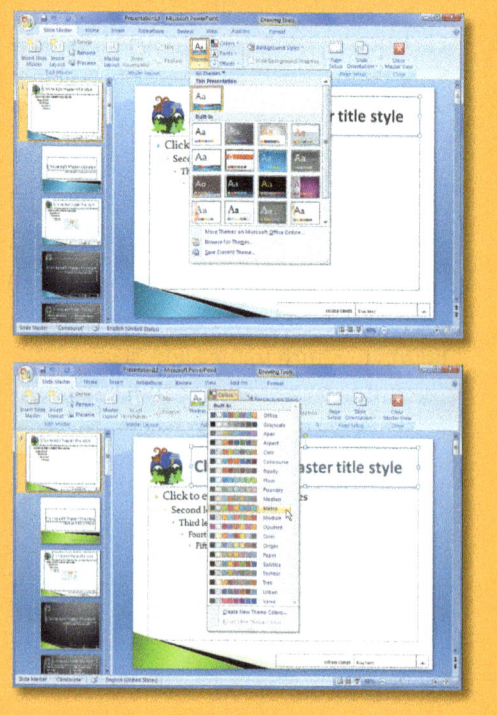

Multimedia exercise 16

Using the master

Now that you have a master background, each slide you add to the presentation will have the elements you applied.

1. Think about the last camp you attended with your school, or even a camping holiday with family or friends, or you can simply make it up as you go along!
2. On the Title slide, give the presentation the name of the location where you camped.
3. Add three or four new slides with a Title and Content layout and use each to present information about:
   - where you stayed – location and facilities
   - what you did – excursions, etc.
   - highlights of the camp.

Multimedia exercise 17

Movie Promo Master

The Time Warp Video store has a permanent slide show running in the store that displays new releases. You are to create a master that can be used so that each slide has a consistent look.

1. Start a new presentation and save it in your student folder with the name **Movie Promo**.
2. Apply a background.
3. Put a star in each corner.
4. Put the name of the video store in the bottom footer.

Multimedia exercise 18

Creating a master for the zoo

You can use your own design. This example has resized and placed the placeholders for the title and text as shown. Clip Art has been added and two boxes drawn and shaded for a background.

MODULE 5

Movie clips

Inserting movie clips into a presentation can add a lot of impact. Movie clips can be set to play only when clicked, which adds to the interactive nature of the presentation.

Inserting a movie file

You can easily add a movie file that you have recorded or downloaded from the internet or from another program. You can enter movie clips into a PowerPoint slide show so that it runs either automatically or when selected.

Multimedia exercise 19

Movie clips

1. Start a **New** blank presentation with a Title layout.
2. Enter the text **My Movies** in the title.
3. Save the presentation in you student folder with the name **My Movies**.
4. Add a **New slide** with a blank layout.
5. Click on the **Insert** tab then click on the **Movies** drop list button and click on **Movie from file**.
6. Locate the movie file you want to use and click on **OK**.
7. A prompt will appear asking to check if you want the movie to start automatically when the slide is displayed or only when it is clicked.

   Click on **Automatically**.

   The movie clip will be inserted on the slide. You can also make custom settings. For example, to loop continuously while the slide is displayed.

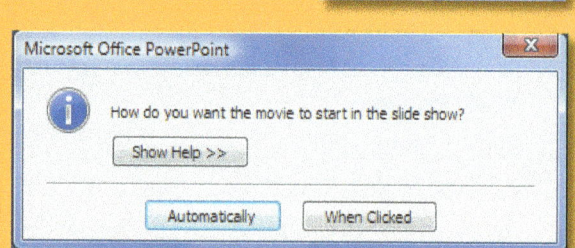

8. Click on the **Preview** button in the **Options** tab.

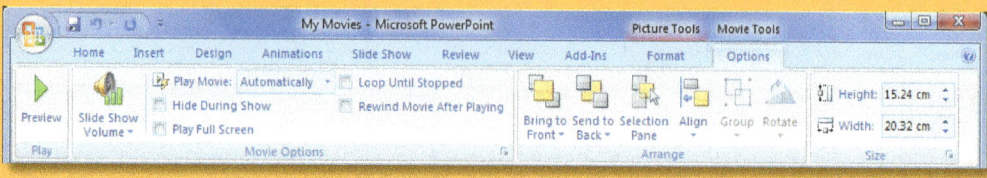

9. Add another slide with a blank layout.
10. Insert another movie clip.
11. Repeat the previous two steps until you have six slides with movie clips.

    Note: There are animated clips available in the Microsoft Clip Art gallery, however, they do not have the same properties as movies (i.e. the Movie Tools Options tab will not appear for an animated clip from the Clip Art gallery).

Action buttons

Action buttons can display various slides within a presentation, causing a program to start, play a sound or movie, link to a webpage and so on. In a simple presentation, they can be useful for displaying a slide that may only be used in particular circumstances. You may have used some programs or Help screens in the past that use a Next, Previous, Start or Finish button.

Action buttons are simply a method of placing navigation buttons on a slide. Before we assign action buttons, we will first create a new presentation.

Image Quality
A mega pixel is the unit of measure of image quality. The higher the number of pixels the better the image will be.

Zoom
A camera can have a digital or optical zoom.
- Optical zoom brings the object of the photo closer by magnifying it before taking the digital image. The result is a better image.
- Digital zoom actually zooms in on the digital image to enlarge it.

Battery
- Standard batteries are used in some cameras which enables you to carry replacements with you. They do not last as long but are cheap and easily replaced.
- Rechargeable batteries are used by some cameras. These batteries last longer but cost much more. They also require access to a power source and a battery recharger.

Memory
- The more memory you have the more photos you can take provided the battery holds out.
- Most cameras can have additional memory inserted.

You will create a button on each slide that enables you to go to the first, previous, next or last slide.

 **Multimedia exercise 20**

1. Start a new presentation and enter the text as shown on the previous page.
2. Save the presentation as **Choosing a Digital Camera**.

Creating action buttons

1. Create an **End** button.
   a. Display the second slide.
   b. Click on the **Insert** tab then click on the **Shapes** button. The **Action buttons** are at the end of the Shapes list.

   Action Buttons

   c. Click on **Action Button: End**.
   d. Click, hold and drag to form a small square at the lower right of the slide.
   e. Click on **OK**.

2. Create a **Next** button.
   a. Click on the **Shapes** button on the Insert tab.
   b. Click on **Action Button: Forward or Next**.
   c. Click, hold and drag to form a small square at the lower right of the slide just before the End button.
   d. Click on **OK**.

3. Create a **Back** button.
   a. Click on the **Shapes** button on the Insert tab.
   b. Click on **Action Button: Back or Previous**.
   c. Click, hold and drag to form a small square at the lower right of the slide just before the Next button.
   d. Click on **OK**.

   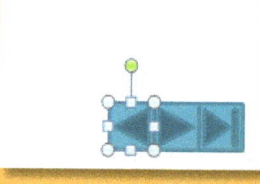

4. Create a **Beginning** button.
   a. Click on the **Shapes** button on the Insert tab.
   b. Click on **Action Button: Beginning**.
   c. Click, hold and drag to form a small square at the lower right of the slide just before the **Back** button.
   d. Click on **OK**.

   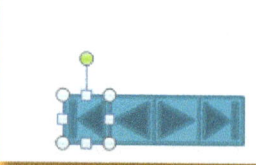

5. Repeat this process to create a set of buttons on each slide as appropriate. For example, the last slide would have only a Beginning and Previous button on it.
6. Test the result by running the Slide Show and using the action navigation buttons to move around the presentation.

Creating a custom action button

The custom action buttons are great for creating a menu to specific slides. You will add a new slide that will act as a menu to the remaining slides. You will create a button from the menu slide to each of the remaining slides.

Multimedia exercise 21

Creating a custom action button

1. Open the file called **Activities**.
2. Display the first slide.
3. Click on the **New Slide** button and choose a title and content layout.
4. Add the text as shown, removing the bullets and adjust the layout:
5. Click on **Insert tab** then the **Shapes** button.
6. Click on **Action Button: Custom**.
7. Click, hold and drag to form a small square next to the text.

   The Action Settings dialog box appears. Here you set what happens when the button you have just placed on the slide is clicked.

8. Click on the drop-down button for **Hyperlink** to and click on **Slide**.
9. Click on the slide, in this case **3, Canoeing**, then **OK** and then **OK** again.

   Now, if you click on this button in the slide show, the linked slide is displayed.

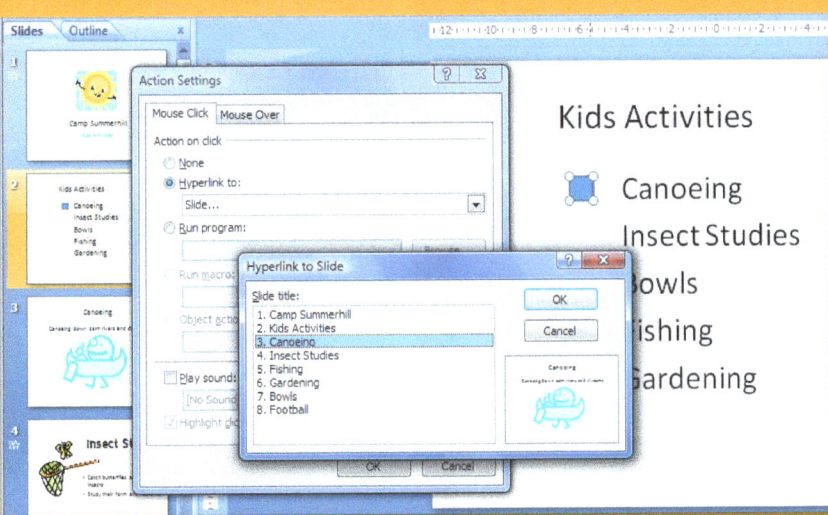

10. Repeat this process to assign each of the options on the second slide to a button.
11. On each slide, create an action button that will return the user to the second slide – use the **Action Button: Custom**.
12. For each of these buttons, use the **Text Box** tool on the **Insert** tab to add the text '**Return to Main Menu**'.
13. Run the slide show to test your buttons.

MODULE 5

Multimedia exercise 22

Adding more hyperlinks

1. Open the file called **Facilities**.
2. Insert a slide after the first slide.
3. Create buttons with hyperlinks to each slide, as described in exercise 21.

Multimedia exercise 23

Using action objects to navigate

1. Create the following slides that provide information on the digestive system.
2. Save the presentation in your student folder with the name **Food for thought**.

The Digestive System

The Digestive Tract
- The Mouth
- The Stomach
- The Small Intestine
- The Oesophagus
- The Liver
- The Large Intestine

The Mouth
- This is where digestion begins
- Chewing physically breaks down food
- Saliva contains an enzyme that chemically breaks down starch
- Saliva also helps the chewing and swallowing actions

The Oesophagus
- This is a hollow muscular tube which leads to the stomach
- Muscular contractions push the food down to the stomach (even if you are standing on your head)

The Stomach
- The stomach churns and mixes food
- Enzymes in the stomach start the digestion of protein
- Hydrochloric acid is also released which will kill bacteria and get the enzymes working

The Small Intestine
- Seven meters long coiled up
- Small molecules resulting from the digestive process pass through the wall into the blood vessels to be carried throughout the body
- Starch and protein digestion are completed
- Fat digestion occurs

Instead of inserting action buttons you can use other drawing shapes.

3 Insert action buttons on each main element that will provide a link to the associated slide.
4 Insert action buttons on each of the slides that explain the digestive elements to return to the main slide.
5 Test your presentation to check that it works correctly.
6 Save and close your presentation.

 Multimedia exercise 24

Proceeding with action buttons
1 Open the file you created earlier called My Movies.
2 Create action buttons on each slide so the user can move through the slides from start to finish. However, they should also at any time be able to return to the first slide or go directly to the last slide to finish.

Multimedia project 1

The Sorrento is a hotel located on the Gold Coast of Australia. There are three standards of room available for two people: Supreme – $200 per night; Deluxe – $150 per night and Poolside – $100 per night. Facilities include a fabulous heated pool and spa with views to the ocean, fully equipped gym, valet parking, room service, laundry and a restaurant for dinner and buffet breakfast. Apart from glorious beaches, the surrounding attractions are nearby mountains, theme parks, shopping and the theatre centre, there are also day trips and activities such as snorkelling, trail riding, water skiing and markets. Room bookings can be made by contacting Hayley by telephone on (07) 5647 3333 or fax (07) 5647 4444, or email rooms@sorrento.com.au.

Your brief is to create a presentation that provides details about the hotel. The hotel is decorated in marine colours and white so incorporate these into the colours of the presentation.

Investigate the problem

Look at designs available in PowerPoint. Gather images and photos that will be used in the presentation.

Design the solution

Sketch a design of each slide on paper, including possible graphics to illustrate the slides and text that will be entered on each slide.

You should plan to include:
- title slide
- menu slide
- slides on each feature of the motel: rooms, facilities, surrounding attractions, bookings
- the facilities slide could be a sub-menu that branches to each of the facilities and an explanation of each.

Produce the solution

Use the PowerPoint program to produce the solution.

Evaluate the solution

Ask other people to look at your presentation and give you feedback on how effective it is. Summarise what was said and the changes you made to your presentation because of their comments.

Multimedia project 2

Cinemania is a club of movie enthusiasts. They are always keen to have new members. They have decided to create a presentation that can be viewed at the local cinema or on the cinema website. Your brief is to create a presentation that provides details about the group.

Membership costs $60 per year. On joining, you receive a book of movie money worth $50, a very stylish Cinemania cap and a voucher for dinner for two at the restaurant next door to the cinema, the View Grand. Once a month the club holds a free screening of the movie of the month, after which they adjourn to the restaurant next door for free coffee and cake.

Investigate the problem

Look at designs available in PowerPoint. Gather movie clips and images that will be used in the presentation.

Design the solution

Sketch a design of each slide on paper, including possible graphics to illustrate the slides and text that will be entered on each slide.

You should plan to include:
- title slide
- menu slide
- slides on each feature of the group:
  – benefits of being a member
  – membership cost
  – fund-raising activities – a sub-branch to three specific activities and details
  – movie of the month – a sub-branch of the last three movies of the month.

Produce the solution

Use the PowerPoint program to produce the solution. The user should be able to navigate around the presentation. The presentation should incorporate a master so it can be used again for further presentations.

Evaluate the solution

Ask other people to look at your design and give you feedback on how effective it is. Summarise what was said and the changes you made to your design because of their comments.

The different types of graphics programs

Graphics programs allow you to create your own sketches or make changes to existing sketches. There are two main types of graphics programs: bitmapped or pixel-based programs; and object-oriented or vector-based programs.

Bit-mapped or pixel-based programs

These are commonly called **Paint** programs and are used for artistic painting or freehand drawing. The painting is created by the program turning screen lights (called pixels) on or off or to colours. Some common pixel-based programs are Adobe Photoshop, the Painting section of AppleWorks and Microsoft Paint. Pixel-based programs require a larger amount of disk space to store their files.

Object-oriented or vector-based programs

These are commonly called **Drawing** (or computer-aided design) programs and are used when accurate measurements or files of smaller size are required. The drawing is created by drawing a series of straight lines between given points (vectors). Drawing programs are commonly used for architectural drawing. Some common vector-based programs are Adobe Illustrator, CorelDraw, AutoCAD, AutoSketch, ArchiCAD and Deneba CAD. Vector-based programs require less disk space to store files than pixel-based programs.

Some programs, such as Adobe Photoshop and Adobe Fireworld, combine pixel and vector-based techniques.

Creating a painting

In the next exercise, you will be following a set of steps to create the sketch of a fishing rod in a stream next to a rock, shown below. Once the sketch is complete, save it and print a copy of it in colour if a colour cartridge is available. The notes have been developed for Microsoft Paint, but other Paint programs could be used.

MODULE 6

computer graphics

Computer graphics exercise 1

Skills practised:

Drawing tools

Filling

Shading

Spray painting

Saving

Printing

Creating a painting

1 Use the Pencil tool to draw a rock shape near the bottom centre of the screen.

2 Draw a thicker curved line to the left of the rock to create the edge of the stream and add blue shading next to it using the Airbrush or Brush tools.

3 Add some green shading along the edge of the stream, beneath the rock and behind the rock.

4 Use the Fill with colour tool to fill the rock with a light and dark shade of grey then Spray over the rock and edge of the stream with light brown.

5 Use the Line tool to draw a blanket next to the grass below the rock then use the Rounded Rectangle tool to draw a basket.

6 Use the Fill with colour tool to fill the basket with a pattern or colour then fill the blanket with a different pattern or colour.

7 Use the Oval tool to draw some blue ovals in the stream then use the Line tool to draw the rod and line from the blanket to the stream.

8 Use the Polygon or Line tools to draw some mountains above the rock then use the Line tool to enclose the mountains.

9 Fill the mountains with a shade of grey or brown. Save your sketch and print a copy.

Making a more detailed sketch

Use the steps in the next exercise to create a sketch of a fish swimming next to a rock, as shown. Once the sketch is complete, save it and print a copy of it in colour if a colour cartridge is available.

 **Computer graphics exercise 2**

Making a more detailed sketch
Creating the fish

1. Use the Ellipse or Oval tools to drawn an orange oval shape filled with white near the centre of the screen. This is the fish's body.

   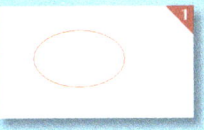

2. Use the Polygon tool to create a fin at the top of the fish's body.

3. Add two more fins (polygons) at the lower side of the body and at the end.

4. Use the Pencil tool to create the head of the fish.

5. Fill the head with a solid orange colour, fill the body with an orange pattern or colour and fill the fins with yellow.

6. Add some orange lines through the fins and add a small white circle in the head to represent the eye.

7. Add a small black circle in the white circle to represent the eyeball.

8. Use the Pencil tool to draw a small arc underneath the eye to represent the mouth.

Adding the background

1. Use the Brush tool (or Pencil) to drawn an ocean bed in yellow below the fish.

2. Use the Pencil tool to add some grey and brown rocks on the ocean bed.

3. Fill the ocean bed with yellow and the rocks with grey and brown.

4. Use the Brush tool to add some green plants near the rocks.

5. Use the Brush tool to add some blue wavy lines at the top of the screen then use the Line or Brush tools to enclose the screen at both sides.

6. Fill the wavy lines with a dark blue then fill the rest of the enclosed shape with a lighter blue to represent the ocean.

7. Use the Air Brush tool to add some white spray to the dark blue section at the top of the ocean.

Copying graphics

Shapes drawn in painting programs can be copied and pasted as often as required. The graphic must be selected either by using the **Edit Marquee** (Edit Box) or the **Lasso** tool. The difference between the two is that the Edit Marquee places a rectangular frame around the shape, whereas the Lasso tool selects the shape itself.

The Edit Marquee or Select tool places a rectangular frame with white space around the shape.

The Lasso or Free-Form Select tool just selects the shape of the object.

 **Computer graphics** *exercise 3*

Copying graphics

1. From your school's Clip Art library, find a picture of a house and insert it onto the Paint program's screen.
2. Insert a picture of a tree next to the house.

3. Use the Lasso or Free-Form Select tool to enclose the tree, click on the Transparent Background button (bottom button) and copy it (Edit menu – Copy, or press Ctrl+C or ⌘+C).
4. Paste the tree and move the copies next to the left of the house so that they overlap one another.

5. Some paint programs allow you to hold down the Ctrl or Option key and drag a selected object to make a copy of it. Try it, or copy and paste to add trees to the right side of the house.

6. Try inserting some trees using the Edit Marquee or Select tool to select the tree. The white space around the tree will mean that the effect is not what is desired.

Skills practised:

Using the Edit Marquee

Using the Lasso tool

Copying

Pasting

Editing graphics

Most Painting programs provide you with a range of tools to alter the appearance of graphics. Some of these include flipping, rotating, scaling (resizing), inverting, slanting and distorting, among others.

 **Computer graphics** exercise 4

Skills practised:

Using the Edit Marque

Rotating

Flipping vertically

Flipping horizontally

Inverting

Distorting

Using perspective

Resizing

Editing graphics

1. Insert a picture from your school's Clip Art library onto the Painting screen.
2. Place the Edit Marquee or Select tool around the picture.
3. Use Flip/Rotate from the Image menu to carry out each of the following transformations.

   a. Rotate by 90° – the shape should rotate 90° to the right.

   b. Flip Vertical. The shape is turned upside down.

   c. Flip Horizontal. The shape is flipped to face the opposite horizontal position.

   d. Invert. The colours are altered to their opposite colour.

   e. Stretch. One side of the shape is stretched.

   f. Skew. Two sides of the shape are altered to give a 3-D effect.

4. Try changing the shape's Attributes to make the shape smaller.
5. Try changing the shape's Attributes to make the shape larger. Sometimes increasing the size of a shape can cause its definition (accuracy) to be decreased.

Introduction to photo editing

When you work with photographs, a more professional graphics program is required. Adobe Photoshop, Adobe Photoshop Elements and Adobe Fireworks are some examples of suitable programs.

The following exercises have been prepared using Adobe Photoshop Elements, which is an education version of Adobe Photoshop with all the necessary photo-editing features. You will need access to the PIT Book 1 Support Files, which can be downloaded from the Cambridge University Press website (www.cambridge.edu.au/educaton/PIT). You may need to ask your teacher for the location of the files.

 **Computer graphics exercise 5**

Skills practised:

Blur tool

Sharpen tool

Sponge tool

Dodge tool

Burn tool

Gradient tool

Opening a sample photograph

1. Start Adobe Photoshop Elements and click on Browse for File.
2. Access the PIT Book 1 Support Files.
3. Open the Venice file. This is a photograph of Venice that needs some improvements made to it.

Photo-editing tools

Numerous photo-editing tools are provided in Photoshop Elements. The most frequently used are displayed in the Drawing tools at the left of the screen. You can click on the tool displayed to see the other tools. The tools are labelled in the diagram below.

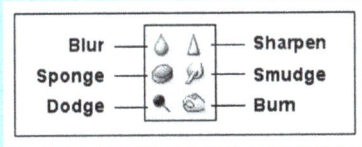

The Blur tool

The Blur tool softens hard edges or areas in an image to reduce detail.

1. Select the Blur tool in the Drawing tools. Its options are displayed in a toolbar at the top of the screen.
2. Click on the arrow next to the left box in the toolbar (the Brush Presets). Set the Brushes box to Default Brushes and click on the first 9 pt Brush style. There are hundreds of brushes and sizes available.

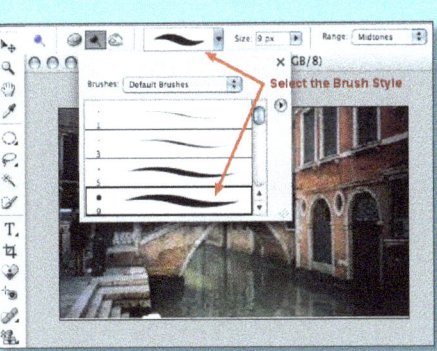

3. Try painting over the small piece of sky at the top centre of the photograph. This blurs the colours together.
4. Click on the Undo Blur tool from the Edit menu (or press Ctrl+Z or ⌘+Z) to undo the blur effect.
5. Try selecting different Modes from the toolbar at the top of the screen and paint over the sky to observe the different blur effects. Undo any effects that you do not like.

The Sharpen tool

The Sharpen tool enhances soft edges to increase clarity.

1. Select the Sharpen tool and in its toolbar set the Brush Preset back to the first 9 pt style. Set the Mode to Saturation to allow areas to be shown in more detail.
2. Zoom in on the photo by holding down the Ctrl key on the Windows system or the ⌘ key on the Macintosh and pressing the + key.
3. Paint lightly over the people on the bridge. The more you paint, the sharper the image becomes. Remember, you can always press Ctrl+Z or ⌘+Z to undo any steps.
4. Zoom out by pressing Ctrl+ – or ⌘+ –.
5. Experiment with other sharpen modes.

The Sponge tool

The Sponge tool subtly changes the colour saturation or vividness of an area.

1. Select the Sponge tool from the Drawing tools.
2. In the toolbar, set the Mode box to Saturation (this intensifies the colour).
3. Try painting over the building at the right of the photograph to increase its colour intensity.

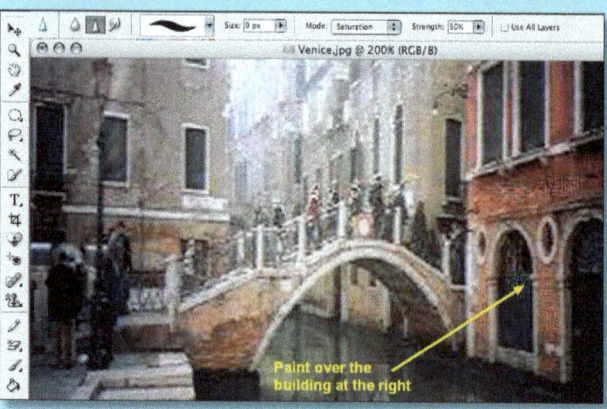

The Smudge tool

The Smudge tool merges existing colours or smears new colours into an image.

1. Select the Smudge tool. Select the 9 pt brush and set the Mode to Normal.
2. Paint over the water area to merge the colours.
3. Experiment with the other Modes for the Smudge tool.

The Dodge and Burn tools

The Dodge tool lightens areas of an image; the Burn tool darkens areas. There are three Ranges (or settings) for these tools: Midtones to change the middle range of greys, Shadows to change the dark areas and Highlight to change the light areas.

1. Select the Dodge tool then set the Size box in the toolbar to about 16 pt and the Range box to Midtones.
2. Paint over the left side of the photograph to lighten its midtones.

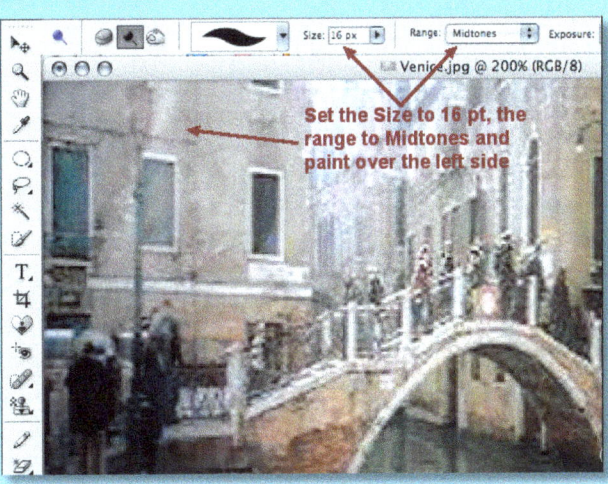

3. Try setting the Range to Shadows and paint over an area. The dark areas are made much lighter. Remember, you can undo any unwanted effects.
4. Try setting the Range to Highlights and paint over an area. The light areas are made much lighter. Then select undo.

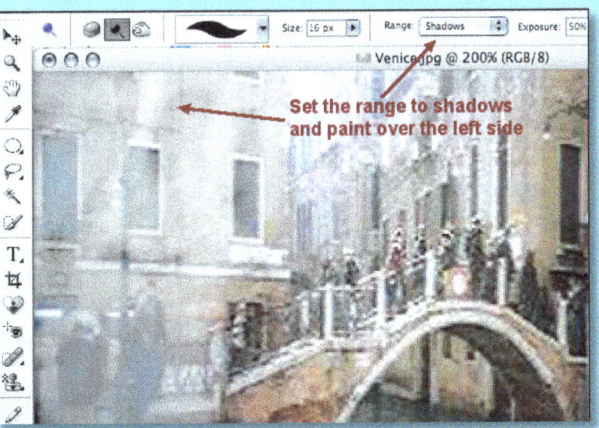

143

5. Select the Burn tool and set the Size box in the toolbar to about 16 pt.
6. Paint over the right side of the photograph to darken its midtones.
7. Try using the other two ranges.

Gradient fill

Another way to fade a photograph is to apply a gradient fill.

1. Select the Gradient Fill tool from the Drawing tools.
2. At the bottom of the Drawing tools, set the Foreground and Background Colours to white.
3. In the Toolbar, click on the arrows next to the Gradient Picker box and select Foreground to Transparent.

4. Using the pointer, drag a straight line from the centre left of the image to the centre.

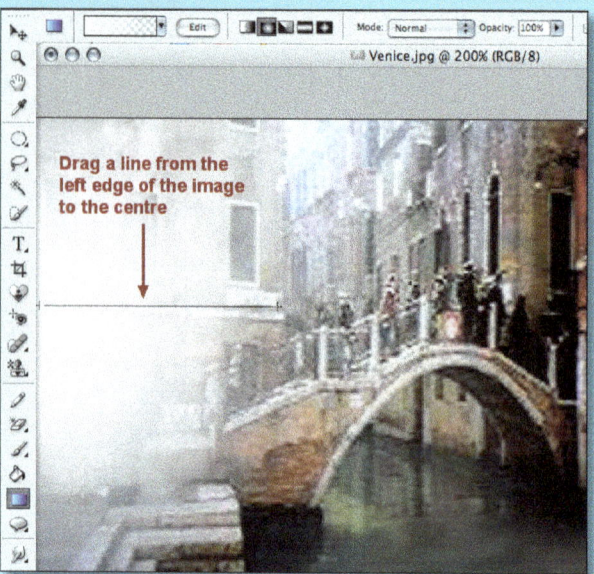

5. Release the mouse button and the image fades to clear.
6. Experiment with other gradient fills, which are next to the Edit button in the toolbar.
7. Display the File menu and click on Save. In the Format box, set the image format to Photoshop PDF. This reduces the size of the file to a more economical size.
8. Access your Storage folder and call the file **Graphics Exercise 5**.
9. Click on OK and you will be asked to set the quality of the file. Select 8, which is ample quality for these purposes and then click OK.

computer graphics

Special effects

Photo-editing programs provide numerous special effects. In this exercise you will apply some of those effects to create a designer pet.

Computer graphics exercise 6

Skills practised:

Distorting images

Liquify effect

Twirl tool

Bloat tool

Warp tool

Special effects

1. Start Photoshop Elements or close any Photoshop Elements files that are open.
2. Display the File menu and click on Open. Access the PIT Book 1 Support Files and open the **Cat** file.
3. Display the Filter menu, highlight Distort and click on Liquify. The image opens in a separate window.
4. Try each of the tools on the left side of the window, painting over the image to see each effect. Click on the Revert button at the right of the window to return the image to its original state after each change.
5. Try using the tools to produce a pet of your own design. For example, the Twirl tools can be used to curve the ears, the Bloat tool to increase the size of the eyes and feet, and the Warp tool to change the body shape, etc.

6. Click on OK when you are happy with the effects. You might like to try some of the other Distort effects (use the Filter menu and highlight Distort).
7. Save the image as a Photoshop PDF file in your Storage folder under the file name **Graphics Exercise 6**.

Combining many photographs into one

Sometimes you cannot fit all the subjects in one photograph. Photo-editing programs allow you to merge photographs together. In this exercise you will merge the following three photographs into one.

 **Computer graphics** *exercise 7*

Skills practised:

Photomerge

Crop tool

Adding a page frame

Selecting the images

1. Start PhotoShop Elements or close any Photoshop Elements files that you have open.
2. Display the File menu, hightlight New and select Photomerge Panorama.
3. Click on Browse and access the PIT Book 1 Support Files in exercise 9.
4. Hold down the Shift key and click on the School1, School2 and School3 files to select all three images.
5. Click on Open, then OK and the files will start to merge. Photoshop Elements should have been able to merge two of the images using the yellow block of stone as a reference. The third photograph will need to be added manually. Click on OK.

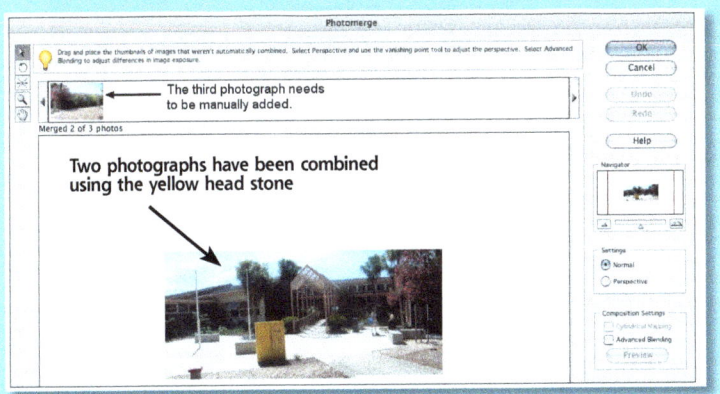

6. Drag the third photograph from the top of the screen to the right of the merged photographs so that the two pieces of concrete in both photos are close to each other. When you release the mouse button the images should snap into place.

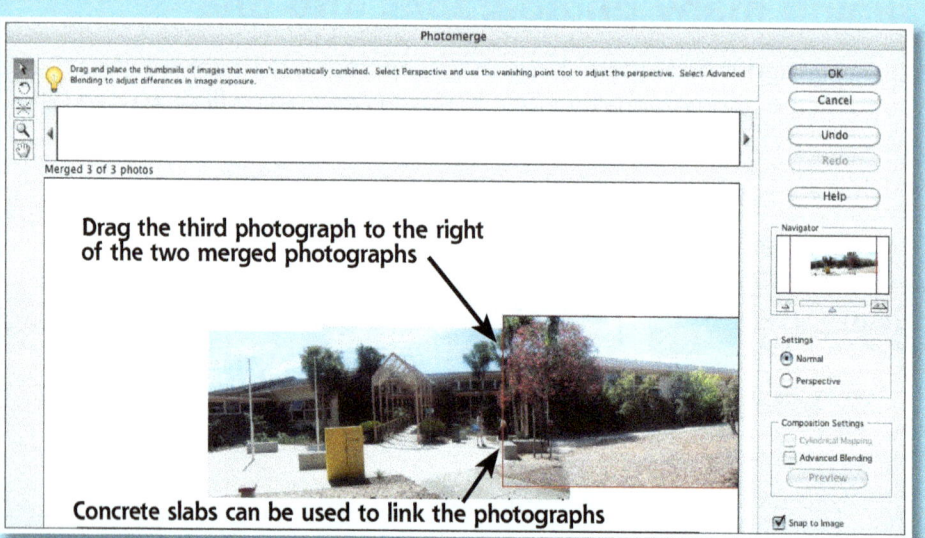

7 Click on OK to combine the images.

Cropping the image

The edges of the photographs don't match perfectly. This problem can be overcome by cropping the image.

1 Press Ctrl– or ⌘– to reduce the zoom to about 16%.
2 Click on the Crop tool from the Drawing tools and drag a frame around the image so that the checkerboard (or transparent) areas are outside the frame.

3 Use the handles to adjust the cropping area if necessary.
4 When you are happy with the position of the cropping frame, double-click inside the frame to delete the parts of the image outside the frame.

Adding a border to the image

Numerous professional borders can be added to the image.

1 In the Styles and Effects palette at the right of the screen, set the top right box to Frames and scroll through the frames that are available.

2 Click on the Brushed Aluminium frame.

3 Drag the frame onto the image and then OK to the Flatten Layers message. The frame should be added to the image.
4 Save the image as a Photoshop PDF file in your Storage folder under the file name **Graphics Exercise 7**.

 Computer graphics **exercise 8**

Using masks

Layers are one of the most fundamental aspects of Photoshop Elements. They allow you to break a drawing up into small selections, which makes detailed drawings much easier to manage. In this exercise you will use layers to create a mask to cover the background of an image. Layers basically fall into three types. One with a white background, one with a coloured background and another with a transparent (or clear) background.

Skills practised:

Using layers

Naming layers

Combining files

Grouping layers

Creating masks

Blur effects

Creating a transparent layer

1 Click on the New button in the toolbar to start a new file.
2 Call the file **Masks**, set the **Width** and **Height** to 500 pixels and set the **Background Contents** (layer type) to **Transparent**.

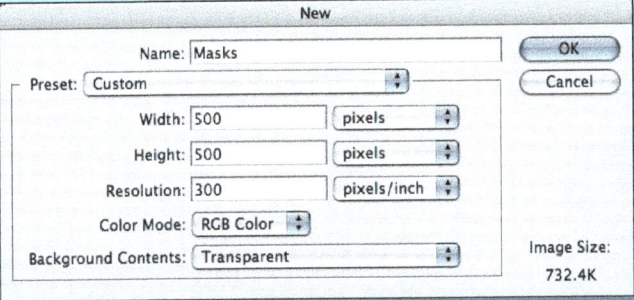

3 Select OK and a page with a speckled background will be created. This represents a transparent page.

Drawing a circular selection area

The Elliptical Marquee will be used to draw a circle in the screen. This will be filled and then become a window to view other pictures.

1 Set the **Edit Marquee Tool** in the toolbar to the **Elliptical Marquee Tool**.

2 Drag an oval selection on the page.

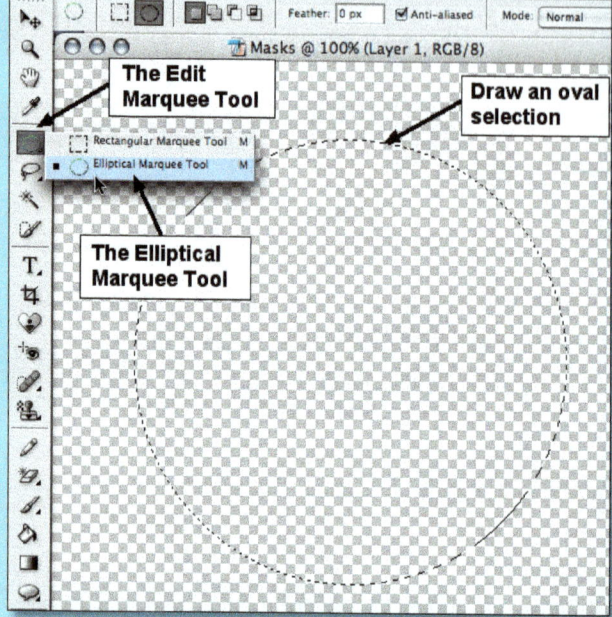

Filling the selection area

In this case the selection area will be filled to black.

1 Display the **Edit** menu and select **Fill Selection**.

2 Set the **Use** box to **Black**.

3 Select OK and the circular selection should be filled to black.

4 Click outside the circle to deselect it.

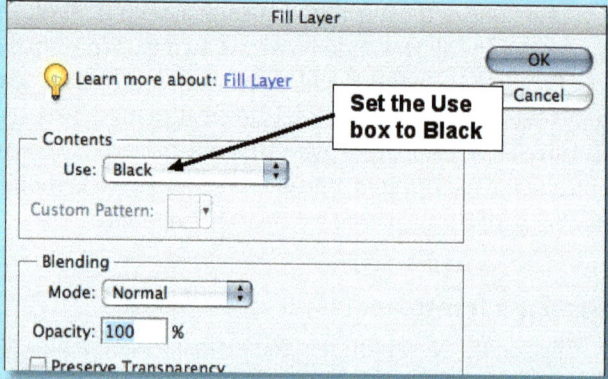

Naming the layer

It is good practice to name layers so that you know what they refer to, particularly when you start creating more detailed documents.

1 Double click on the **Layer 1** label in the **Layers** palette to highlight its name.

2 Enter the name: Mask

Adding a background file

A picture of a dog will be used as the background image.

1. Open the **Dog** image from the PIT Book 1 Support files.

2. Move the Dog window so that you can see both the Mask and the Dog files.

3. Move the mouse over the **Background** layer name in the **Dog** file and drag it onto the **Mask** file.

4. A layer should be added above the Mask layer. Name the new layer **Background**.

5. With the Background layer still selected, display the **Layer** menu and select **Group With Previous** to combine the Background layer with the Mask layer.

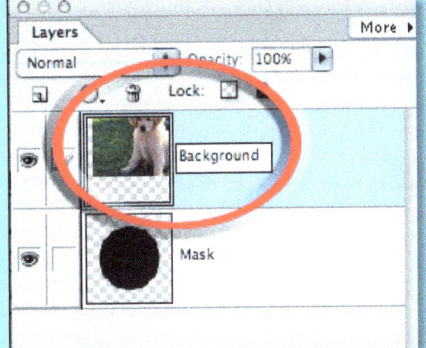

6. An arrow will be added to the Background layer and it will be indented to indicate that it is combined with the MASK layer. The Mask layer is underlined to indicate that it is the host layer.

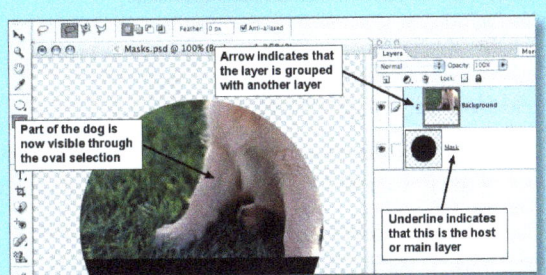

7. You will notice that you can now see part of the dog through the Foreground layer. The background can only be seen where pixels have been drawn in the transparent layer.

8. Select the **Move** tool from the **Toolbar** and you should be able to drag more of the dog into view in the oval.

Blurring the mask

A blur effect can be added to the mask to produce a photo effect.

1. Select the **Mask** layer in the **Layers** palette then display the **Filter** menu, highlight **Blur** and select **Gaussian** Blur.

2. Increase the **Radius** of the blur to about 14 pixels to add a fade effect to the oval selection.

3. Save the document in your Storage folder as a Photoshop PDF file under the file name **Graphics Exercise 8**.

Note: You can use a custom shape rather than the edit marquee to be the mask. If you do this you can apply layer styles to the shape.

Adding text to images

You can also add text to an image.

 **Computer graphics** exercise 9

Adding text to an image

1. Start a new file and name it **Text**. Set the Width to 800 pixels, the Height to 600 pixels, the Resolution to 72 pixels per inch and Background Contents to White.
2. Click on OK to start the file.
3. Click and hold down the mouse button on the Text tool (T) in the Drawing tools and click on the Horizontal Type tool.
4. In the toolbar at the top of the screen, select a Font Style, a Font Family and set the Font Size to 30 pt.
5. Click near the top left of the screen and enter your first name.
6. Use the mouse to highlight your name and in the toolbar set the Color box to a colour of your choice.
7. Click on the Create Warped Text tool and select the different styles, in turn, from the Style box to see their effect on your name. Refer to the following diagram.

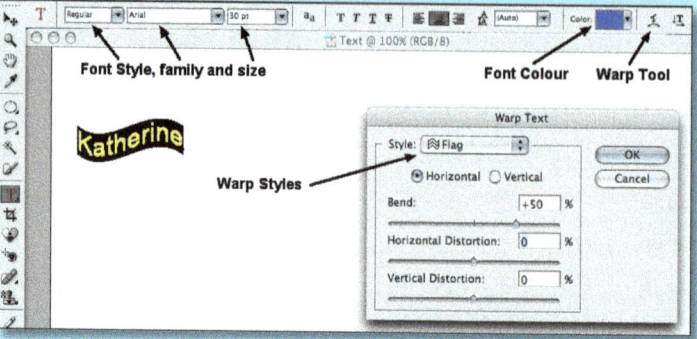

8. Try changing the Horizontal and Vertical Distortion in the Warp Text dialog box.
9. Click on OK to set the text.
10. Click and hold on the Text tool again and click on the Vertical Text tool.
11. Click at the left of the screen and enter your last name. This time the text flows down the screen.
12. Again, you can change the colour and warp the text.
13. To move the text around the screen, click on the Move tool from the Drawing tools. Click on the text box and drag it to its required position.

Computer graphics project

Murrayville Council wishes to advertise the new nature sanctuary that they have just opened and you have been employed to create the page for them. This page could be added to a website, included in a newspaper or simply printed and displayed around the district.

1. Open the **Sanctuary** file from the PIT Book 1 Support Files.
2. Use the photo-editing tools that you have used to fade parts of the photograph and enhance other sections.
3. Add the text shown in the diagram below.
4. Crop the image and add a border to it.

Note: If you need to edit any part of the image, display the **Layers** palette (**Window** menu – **Layers**). Click on the required layer then carry out the edit.

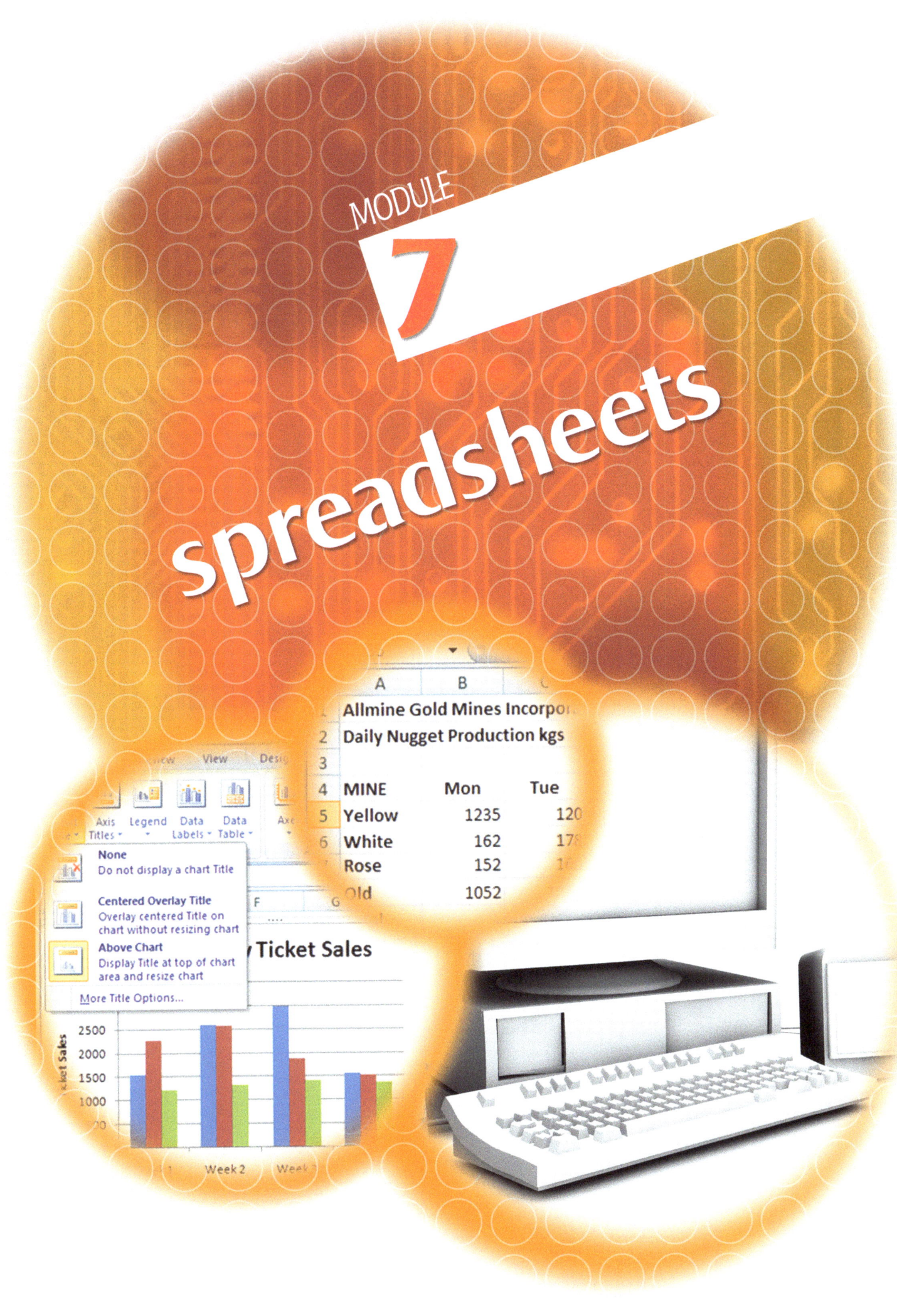

What is a spreadsheet?

A spreadsheet is an application that is used to organise and manipulate data. A spreadsheet is divided into **columns** and **rows**, allowing data to be organised in a systematic manner.

The columns and rows create **cells** that are used to store data and formula.

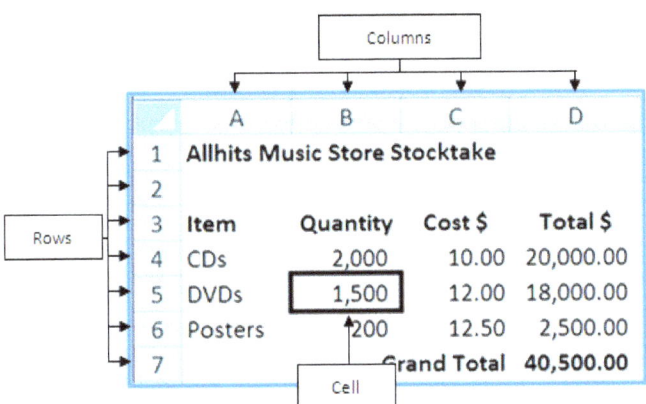

A spreadsheet can be used to:
- list results
- do calculations
- create graphs
- sort information.

While all these tasks can be performed by hand on paper, it is much quicker to use a computerised spreadsheet because it automatically recalculates each time new data is entered or changed.

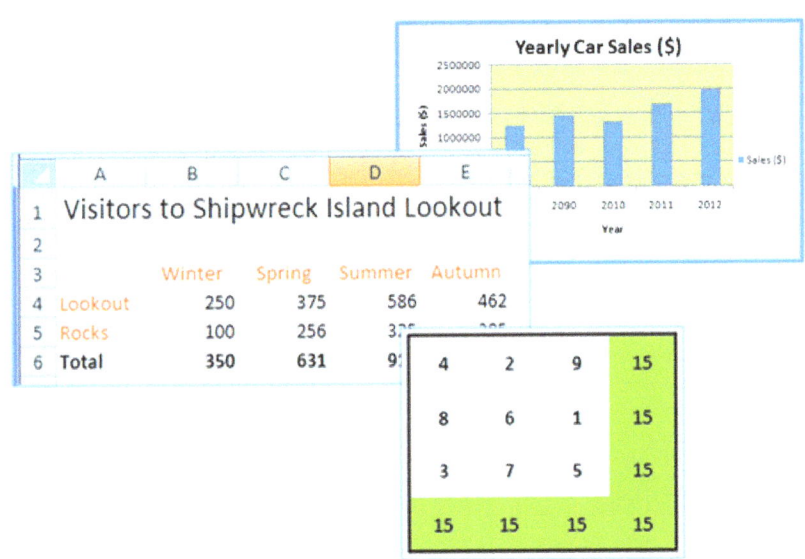

Spreadsheet structure

The intersection of columns and rows in a spreadsheet creates cells. Each cell on a spreadsheet has a name or address. It is named according to its location, the name of the column first followed by the name of the row.

	A	B	C	D
1	Allhits Music Store Stocktake			
2				
3	Item	Quantity	Cost $	Total $
4	CDs	2,000	10.00	20,000.00
5	DVDs	1,500	12.00	18,000.00
6	Posters	200	12.50	2,500.00
7			Grand Total	40,500.00

The **columns** in this spreadsheet are named with **letters**. The **rows** are named with **numbers**. So the first cell in the top left-hand corner is called **A1**. The cell that has the word **CDs** in it is **A4**. The Grand Total value of **40,500.00** is in cell **D7**.

> ### Spreadsheet exercise 1
>
> **Spreadsheet structure**
>
> Look at the spreadsheet above.
> 1. What is the text in cell **A6**?
> 2. What is the name of the cell in which the text **Cost** appears?
> 3. What are the names of all the cells in which the number **12** appears?
> 4. a What is the number in **B5**?
>   b What is the number in **C5**?
>   c What is the result of multiplying these two numbers?
>   d What is the name of the cell in which this number appears?

Skills practised:

Locating cells

Data entry

Spreadsheets can be used simply for entering and organising data.

Spreadsheet exercise 2

Data entry

1. Create the spreadsheet below by entering text and numbers into each cell.

	A	B	C	D	E
1	All Time Top 10 Hits				
2					
3		Title		Artist	
4		1 Imagine		John Lennon	
5		2 Hey Jude		Beatles	
6		3 Hotel California		Eagles	
7		4 American Pie		Don McLean	
8		5 Unchained Melody		Righteous Brothers	
9		6 Bohemian Rhapsody		Queen	
10		7 In the Air Tonight		Phil Collins	
11		8 Down Under		Men at Work	
12		9 Stayin' Alive		Bee Gees	
13		10 You're the Voice		John Farnham	

2. Proofread the text and data to check you have entered it correctly.
3. Select **Save**, access your storage disk or folder, enter the name **Hit list**, click on **Save** or **OK**.
4. Close the file.

Skills practised:

Creating a spreadsheet

Entering data

Saving

Formulas and calculations

A spreadsheet is often used to perform calculations. A spreadsheet can have formulas entered to calculate information for us.

A formula is an equation that calculates a new value from existing values.
For example: 40 + 50 = 90.

The formula is: Add the first number to the second number and display the result.
In a spreadsheet it would look like this:

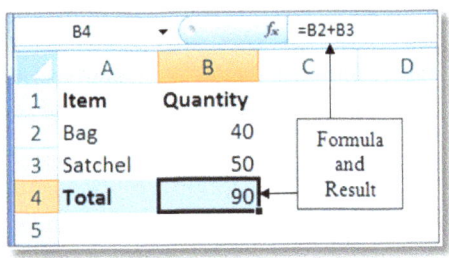

Here are some examples of what spreadsheet formulas can look like:

Subtract   Multiply   Divide
=G6 – G7   =A1*B4   =D5/E5

For example, formulas can be used to calculate the total value of stock in the music store. The number of CDs by the cost of the CDs results in the total value of CDs.

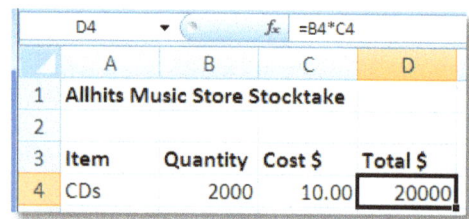

Each formula is entered into the cell that is to display the result. So, in the example above, D4 holds the formula =B4*C4. This will look up the values in cells B4 and C4 and multiply them to give a result, which is then displayed in D4. Microsoft Excel always has an = sign at the start of each formula.

Spreadsheet exercise 3

Simple calculations – multiplication and addition

1. Create the following spreadsheet, entering the text and numbers as shown.

Skills practised:

Creating a spreadsheet

Entering data

Entering formulas

Saving

Format Tip: To make the heading text bold, click on the cell and click on the **Bold** button on the Home tab. To make the cost values have two decimals places, highlight the cells and click on the **Increase Decimal** button until two decimal places are displayed.

2. Proofread the text and data to check you have entered it correctly.
3. Use a formula in cell **D4** that multiplies **B4** by **C4** to give the value of CDs.
4. Repeat to calculate the Total for **DVDs** and another for **Posters**. So you should have a formula in **D4**, another in **D5** and another in **D6**.
5. Put a formula in the cell next to **Grand Total** (**D7**) that will add up the total of each item – that is, add the values in **D4**, **D5** and **D6**.
6. Click on the **Save** button, access your storage disk or folder, enter the name **Stocktake**, click on **Save** or **OK**.

7. Change the cost of CDs to **12.50**. What is the new total for CDs?
8. Change the quantity of **Posters** in **B6** to **256**. What is the new total for posters?

 Spreadsheet **exercise 4**

Skills practised:

Creating a spreadsheet

Entering data

Entering formulas

Saving

Simple calculations – addition

1. Create the following spreadsheet.

	A	B	C	D	E	F	G
1	Allmine Gold Mines Incorporated						
2	Daily Nugget Production kgs						
3							
4	MINE	Mon	Tue	Wed	Thu	Fri	Total
5	Yellow	1235	120	1256	1220	1200	
6	White	162	178	180	179	170	
7	Rose	152	160	162	161	1623	
8	Old	1052	1010	990	999	1022	
9	Total						

2. Use addition to add the total for each day (i.e. each column).
3. Use addition to add the total for each mine (i.e. each row).
4. Select Save, access your storage disk or folder, enter the name **Production**, click on Save.

Challenge – magic square

A 3 x 3 magic square works by entering numbers so all rows, all columns and the diagonal add to the same number.

1. Create a new spreadsheet. (You will learn how to format it to look like the picture later in the module.) Use addition to create a check for the totals on each row, column and diagonal on a magic square. It should work no matter which number it is to add to. Start by entering a solution for 15.

4	2	9	15
8	6	1	15
3	7	5	15
15	15	15	15

2. Test it to add to 21, try it again to add to 20.
3. Save the file as **Magic** and close.

161

MODULE 7

Spreadsheet exercise 5

Skills practised:
- Creating a spreadsheet
- Entering data
- Entering formulas
- Saving

Simple calculations – division and subtraction

1. Create the following spreadsheet.

	A	B	C	D	E	F	G
1	Slice of Heaven Cake Shop						
2					Per Slice:		
3	Item		Cake Cost	Slices	Cost	Price	Profit
4			$		$	$	$
5	Chocolate Mud		40.00	10		6.50	
6	Carrot		24.00	8		4.50	
7	Banana		28.00	8		4.50	
8	Ginger Delight		25.00	10		5.00	
9	Strawberry Cream		33.00	10		6.00	

Format Tip: Highlight the cells and click on the **Center** button on the **Home** tab to centre text and data in a cell.

2. The cost per slice for each cake is the cost of the cake divided by the number of slices into which it is cut. Enter a formula to calculate the cost per slice for each cake.
3. The profit per slice is the charge per slice minus the cost per slice. Enter a formula to calculate the profit per slice for each cake.
4. Which cake makes the most money per slice?
5. Which cake makes the least amount per slice?

Challenge: How do we work out the profit per cake?

1. Enter a formula in column **H** to calculate the profit for each cake if every piece of each cake was sold.
2. Select **Save**, access your storage disk or folder, enter the name **Cake price details**, click on **Save** or **OK**.

Spreadsheet exercise 6

Skills practised:
- Creating a spreadsheet
- Entering data
- Entering formulas
- Saving

Simple calculations – multiplication, addition and subtraction

1. Create the following spreadsheet.

	A	B	C	D	E	F	G
1	Canteen Order Form						
2							
3	Name	Jimmy Jamms					
4	Year	9 Red					
5							
6	Item			Qty	Price	Total	
7					$	$	
8	Cheese sandwiches			2	2.50		
9	Stawberry milk			1	3.00		
10	Red frogs			3	0.10		
11	Apple			1	0.50		
12							
13				Total			
14				Money enclosed		10.00	
15				Change			
16							

2. Enter a formula into **F8** that will calculate the charge for two rounds of cheese sandwiches.
3. Enter formulas into the cells **F9**, **F10** and **F11** to calculate the charges for these items.
4. Enter a formula into **F13** that calculates a total charge for all items ordered.
5. Enter a formula in **F15** that calculates the change depending on what is entered in **F14**.
6. Test your spreadsheet. What happens if Jimmy encloses $20 instead of $10? What happens if he orders three rounds of sandwiches?
7. Select **Save**, access your storage disk or folder, enter the name **Order form**, click on **Save**.
8. **Close** the file.

Spreadsheet **exercise 7**

Skills practised:

Creating a spreadsheet

Entering data

Entering formulas

Saving

The SUM function

Special calculations can be made in Excel using Functions. There are many functions available to use in Excel. A very simple but useful function is the SUM function. You can use it instead of entering a long addition equation. Excel even has a special button you can use to enter it quickly. For example, in the calculation below in G5 where previously:

G5=B5+C5+D5+E5+F5   is the same as   G5=SUM(B5:F5)

1. Open the file **Production** you created in exercise 4 or start a new spreadsheet and enter the text and data shown below.
2. Click on cell G5 and click on the Formulas tab then the AutoSum button. Excel scans above and then to left for values to add. Excel assumes you want to add from B5 to F5, which is correct, press Enter to set the formula.
3. Check you are in cell G6 and click on the AutoSum button again to add the next row of values, check the correct cells are being added together then press Enter.

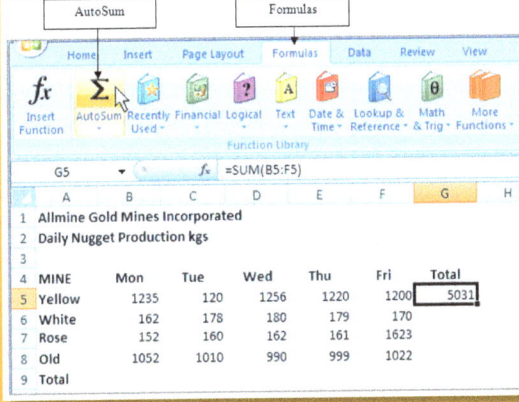

So far so good, however, sometimes the cells you want to add together are not automatically selected.

4. Click into cell G7 and click on the AutoSum button. This time it wants to add the two cells above, which is not what you want. You have to select the correct cells.
5. Highlight the range of cells from B7 to F7, as shown below, then press Enter to set it.
6. Repeat these actions for cell G8.

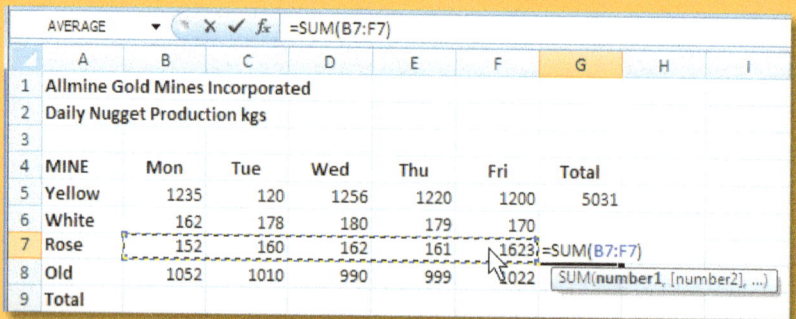

7. Use the AutoSum function to calculate the Total for each day.

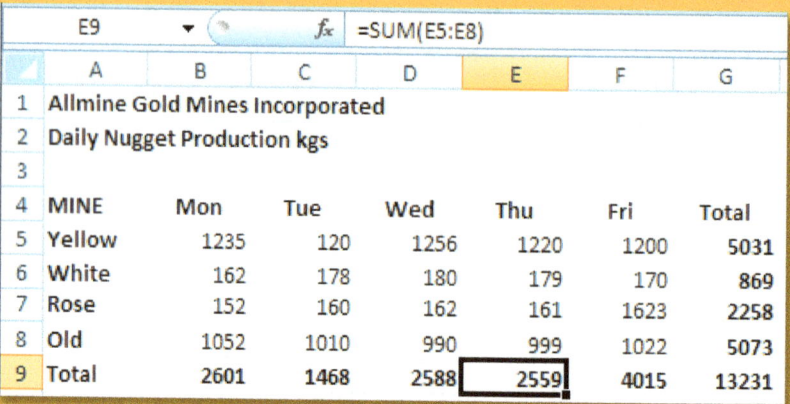

8. Save and close the file.

Formatting

There are lots of ways that the appearance of a spreadsheet can be improved. This is called formatting. The data and text are not actually changed, just the way they appear on the sheet changes. Formatting should make the data in a spreadsheet easier to read. Inserting rows and columns, changing font size and colour, shading cells, formatting numbers and centering text are just some of the formatting features.

Most of the formatting options are available on the Home tab. If you have used Microsoft Word or PowerPoint you will probably be familiar with the buttons that format text size, style and colour.

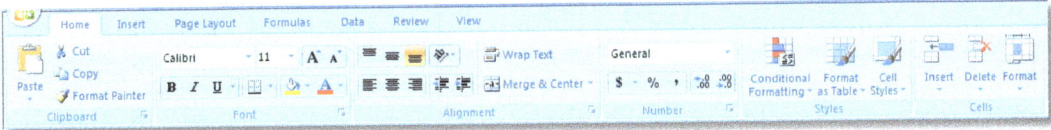

You are going to format the spreadsheet below to look like that on the right.

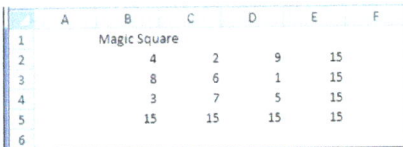
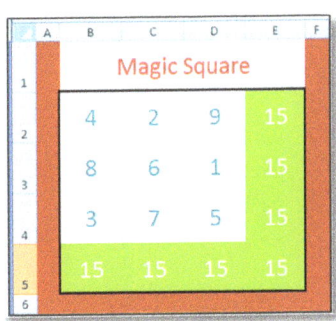

Spreadsheet exercise 8

Formatting

1. Open the file **Magic** created in the challenge for exercise 4 or create it now.
2. Highlight all the cells and click the **Font Size** button and click **20**.
3. Highlight the cells to be filled with colour and click on the **Fill Color** button, select a colour. (You can use the **Theme colors** or click on **More Colors** for more choice.)

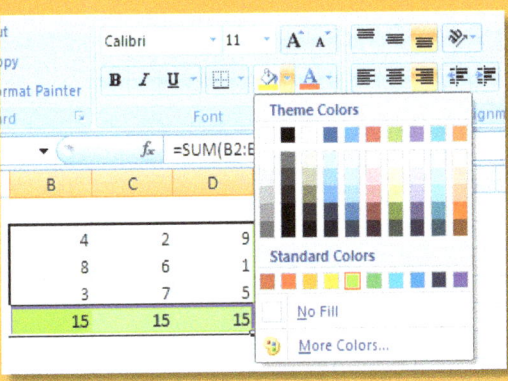

Skills practised:

Creating a spreadsheet

Entering data

Entering formulas

Saving

4   Highlight the cells to have their font colour changed and click on the **Font Color** button and select a colour. Remember, it should be easy to read.

Column width and row height can be modified just by dragging their border.

5   Move the mouse to the lower border of a row to change until the pointer changes to a double-headed arrow. Click, hold and drag down to the required height.

6   Move the mouse over the right hand border of a column to be changed in width until the pointer becomes a double-headed arrow. Click hold and drag.

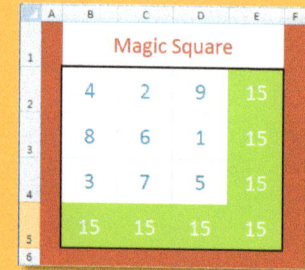

7   A heading can be merged and centred across a range of cells. Select cells B1 to E1 then click on the **Merge & Centre** button on the **Home** tab.

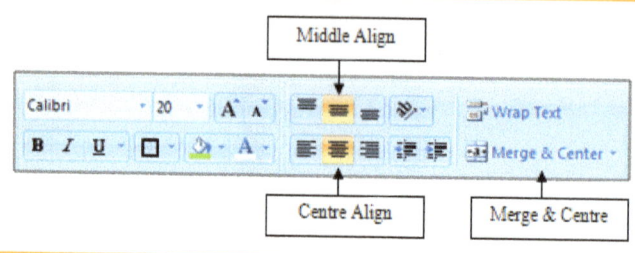

8   Aligning cell contents can be done both vertically and horizontally. Select all the cells then click on the **Middle Align** and **Center** buttons to put all text and data in the centre of each cell.

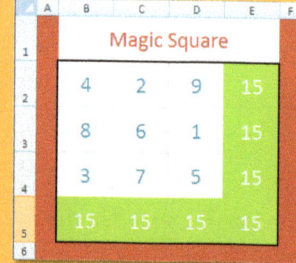

Spreadsheet exercise 9

Skills practised:

Changing font style, size and colour

Aligning

Cell shading

Formatting

1   Open the file **Order form** you created in exercise 6 or create the spreadsheet below.

2   Delete the text in rows 3 and 4, and re-enter it in rows 1 and 2, as shown to the right.

3   Highlight the two rows and click on the **Delete** rows button.

4   Highlight the columns B and C and click on the **Delete** columns button (the same button – just depends on what you have selected).

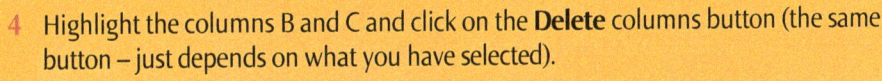

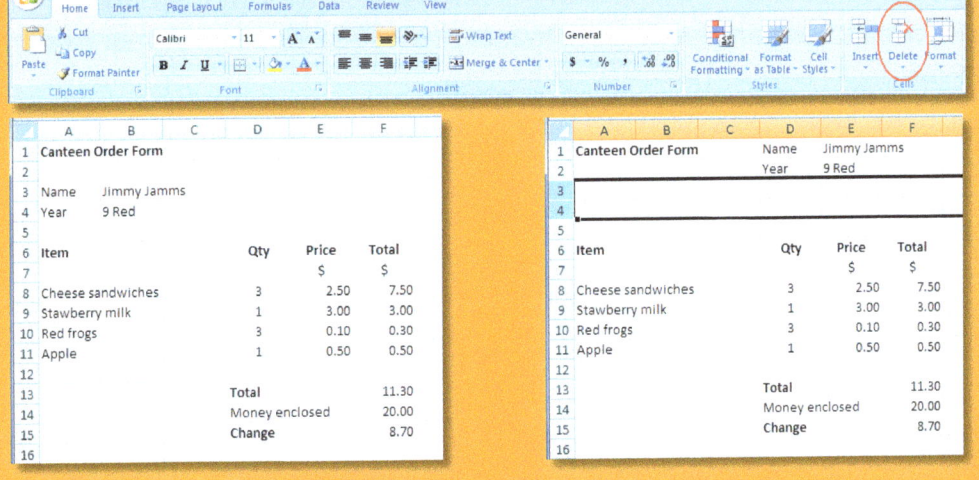

5   The font size and type can be changed to highlight different areas of the spreadsheet. Headings usually have a larger font and can be bold. The colour of data can also be changed. Use Font Size, Type, Color and Alignment to modify the way the list appears.

6   Shading cells can distinguish headings and different areas of the spreadsheet. Shade the headings and columns various colours to distinguish each area.

Extras: Open the file Hit List and format similar to that shown to the right.
Open your other spreadsheet files and format them to look more interesting.

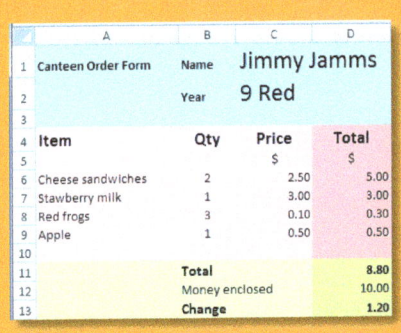

Charts

A chart is a picture of data. An appropriate style of chart can improve the value of data by indicating trends and comparisons. Charting data can make the data more useful. If the right type of chart is chosen, clear trends can be displayed.

The simplest chart is a simple bar chart. The chart must begin with data, for example, a table showing the total sales for the past five years.

	2008	2009	2010	2011	2012
Sales ($)	1256895	1452687	1324568	1687594	1987542

The values in this table can be plotted so that the revenue for each year is clearly displayed. The upward trend in revenue is much clearer in a chart.

A chart is created using an **X-axis** and a **Y-axis**. The **X-axis** is the horizontal axis. In this chart the **years** are the categories on the **X-axis**. The **Y-axis** is used for the measurement of sales.

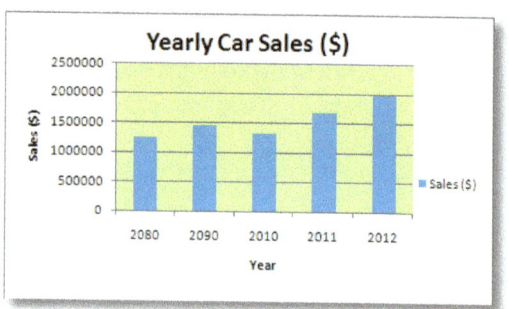

Chart types

There are various chart types that can be used to create charts. The various types give a different view of the data.

The **column** chart is useful for displaying the value of an item or items in a category.

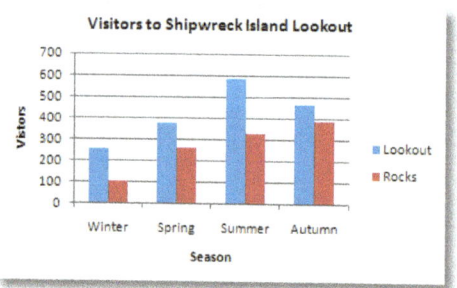

The **line** chart is useful for displaying the relationship between two values. The line chart is used to indicate trends in values.

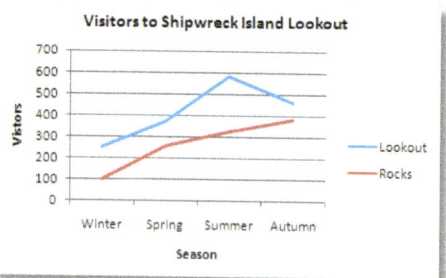

The **pie** chart is useful to compare a small number of values relative to the whole.

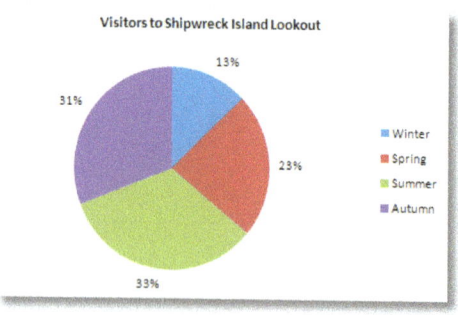

The **area** chart is similar to a line chart with the area below the line filled in.

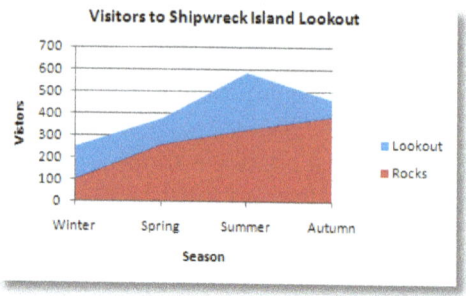

Spreadsheet exercise 10

Skills practised:

Creating a spreadsheet

Entering data

Creating a chart

Saving

Creating a column chart

The local cinema keeps a tally of ticket sales to each film.

1. Create a spreadsheet and enter the data below.

	Week 1	Week 2	Week 3	Week 4
Star Wars	1526	2586	2985	1562
Harry Potter	2246	2568	1864	1502
Crash	1203	1305	1403	1356

2. Select the table of text and data and click on the **Insert** tab then the **Column** button. Select the basic **2-D Column** to create a bar chart that displays the number of ticket sales for each film each week.

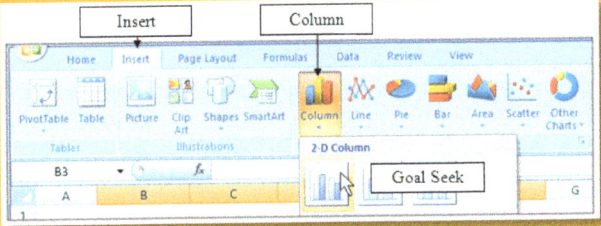

3. With the chart still selected, click on the **Layout** tab, then the **Chart Title** button and select the option **Above Chart**. Type **Weekly Ticket Sales** then press **Enter** to enter a title for the chart.

4. Select **Save**, access your storage disk or folder, enter the name **Films**, click on Save or OK.

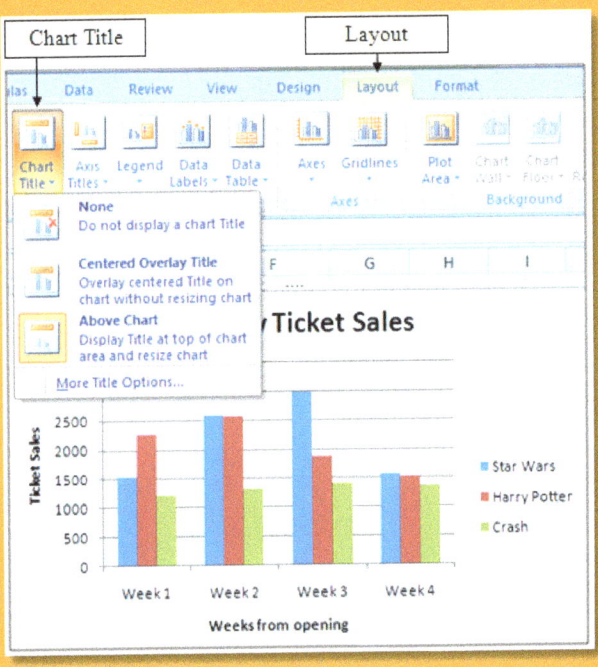

Spreadsheet exercise 11

Skills practised:
- Creating a spreadsheet
- Entering data
- Creating a chart
- Saving

Creating a pie chart

A survey of students revealed the following data about the number of children under 17 living at home.

1. Create a spreadsheet with this data.

No of Children	1	2	3	4 or more
No of Homes	87	152	163	52

2. Create a pie chart that displays the percentage of homes with each category of number of children. Highlight the table, click on the **Insert** tab and click on the **Pie** button, then choose the first **2-D Pie** option.

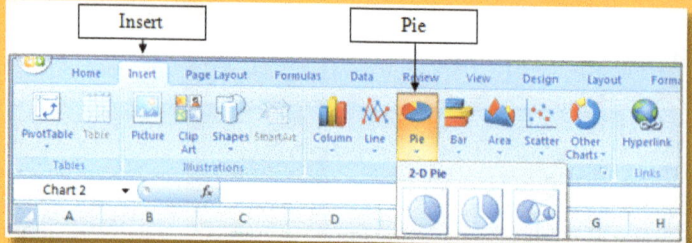

3. The chart will be created with a title. Click into the title and edit the text to read, as shown below.

4. With the chart still selected, click on the **Layout** tab. Click on the **Data Labels** button and the **More Data Labels Options** at the end of the list, click on **Percentage** and **Best Fit** or another of your choice, then click **Close**.

5. Select **Save**, access your storage disk or folder, enter the name **Survey**, click on **Save** or OK.

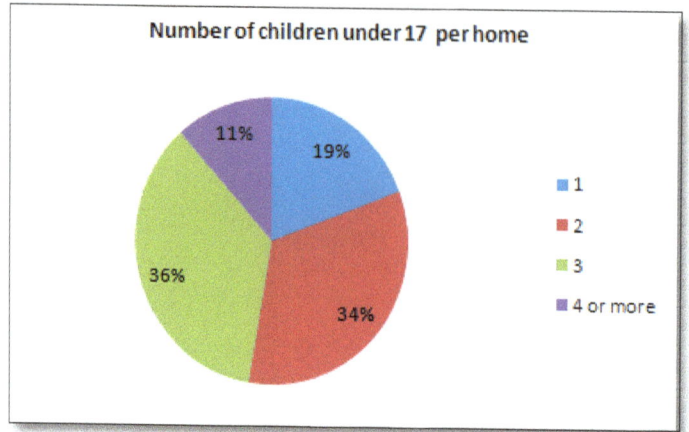

Spreadsheet **exercise 12**

Skills practised:

Creating a spreadsheet

Entering data

Creating a chart

Saving

Creating a bar chart using only part of the data

So far you have used all the data available to create the chart. Sometimes the chart only requires part of the data. In this case you should only select the data you require for the chart.

The spreadsheet below was a result of recording the number of visitors to two locations at a local coastal region.

1. Create this spreadsheet and save it as **Shipwreck** with your student files.

	A	B	C	D	E
1	Visitors to Shipwreck Island Lookout				
2					
3		Winter	Spring	Summer	Autumn
4	Lookout	250	375	586	462
5	Rocks	100	256	325	385
6	**Total**	**350**	**631**	**911**	**847**

2. Create a chart to show the number of visitors to the Lookout each season. (Hint: only select rows 3 and 4 for the data.)

3. Create a chart to show the number of visitors to the **Rocks** each season. (Hint: only select rows 3 and 5 for the data. Select A3 to E3, hold down the **Ctrl** key and select A5 to E5.)

4. Create a chart that includes the number of visitors to each location for each season.

5. Create a pie chart that displays the percentage of total visitors each season.

Using Goal Seek

The **Goal Seek** command is a very useful timesaving measure. For example, Goal Seek can help you calculate the percentage of your pay you should save each week to reach a savings goal.

Spreadsheet exercise 13

Using Goal Seek

In this exercise you will calculate the total savings, given a percentage saved each week. This is suitable for the Goal Seek function, as the result (Total Saved) is directly dependent on the variable (Percentage Saved Weekly).

1. Start a new file and enter the data and text as shown.
2. Use a formula to calculate the amount saved each week and the total saved. The formula in cell **C6** should be **=B6*C3**.

   Suppose you want to save the specific amount of $2000 over 10 weeks. The amount to be earned each week has been estimated and entered. You could experiment with the percentage value to find the level of savings required, or you could use Goal Seek to find the answer in seconds.

3. Click on **C17**, the cell that displays the **Total Saved**. Start here because we know the value for this cell — $2000.
4. Click on the **Data** tab on the ribbon then click on the **What if Analysis** button. Click on the **Goal Seek** option that appears.

Skills practised:

Creating a new spreadsheet

File entering

Formula use

Goal seek function

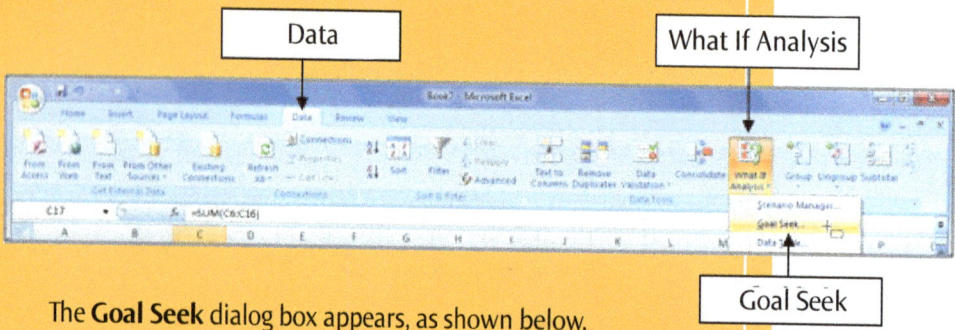

The **Goal Seek** dialog box appears, as shown below.

5. Click in the **To value** box and type **2000** as the amount to be saved.
6. Click in the **By changing cell** box then click on the percentage cell, **C3**, as this is what will need to change to alter the amount saved each week.

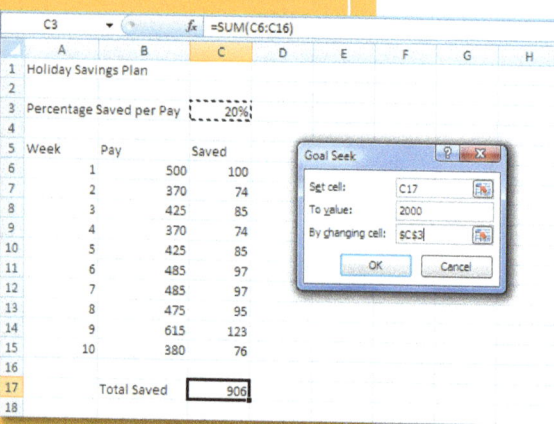

7 Click on **OK**. Goal Seek tries different percentage levels until Total Saved of $2000 would be saved.

   A status message appears when a solution is found.

8 Click on **OK** to accept the search results that are shown below.

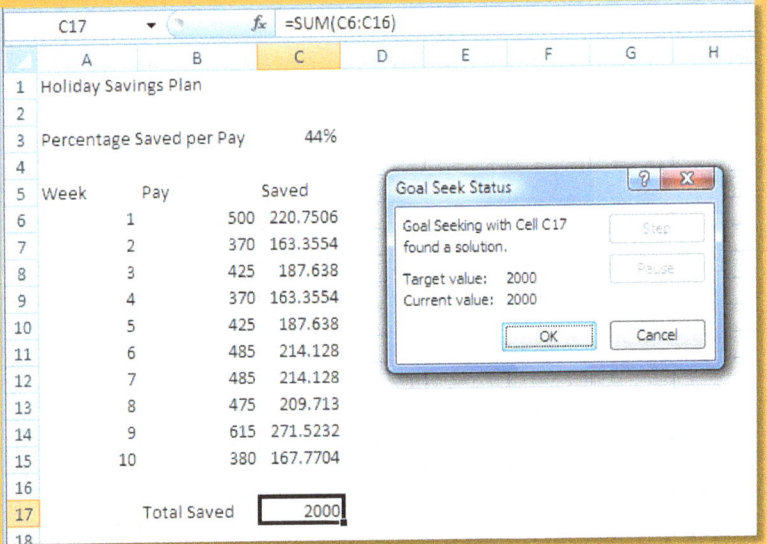

9 Repeat steps 3 to 8 but using $1000 in the **To Value** cell instead of $2000. What is the percentage required now?

10 Repeat the process with other Savings Goals of $5000, $10,000, $100 and $0, etc.

Spreadsheet exercise 14

Using Goal Seek to calculate sales and profit

1 Click on the next blank worksheet tab (e.g. Sheet 2) at the bottom of the window.
2 Create the spreadsheet shown on the following page.
3 Click on cell C5 and enter the formula to calculate **Royalties** =**40%** (B5) multiplied by the **Record Sales (C3)**.
4 Click on cell **C9** and enter the formula for **Profit** = Record Sales (C3) minus the **sum** of Royalties, Production and Promotion Sum (C5:C7).
5 Click on cell **C9**, click on the **Data** tab then the **What if Analysis** button and click on the **Goal Seek** option.

Skills practised:

Creating a new spreadsheet

File entering

Formula use

Goal seek function

6. Use Goal Seek to determine the amount of Record Sales to achieve a Profit of $200,000.

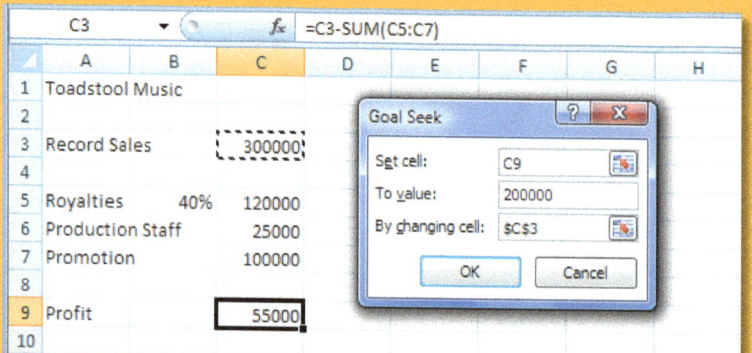

The Goal Seek function searches until it finds a Sales amount so that when 40% is paid in Royalties and the other fixed expenses are taken into account, the Profit will be $200,000.

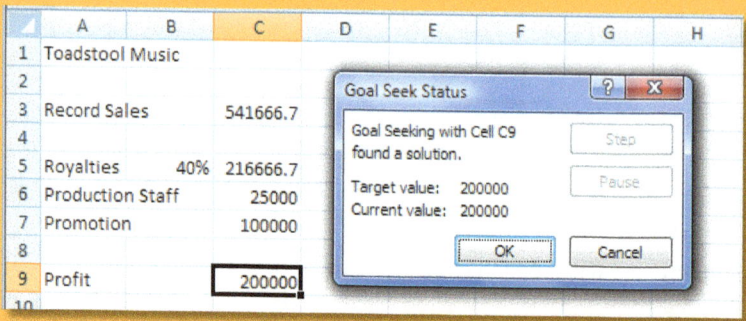

7. Repeat to find the Sales required for a Profit of: $100,000, $300,000, $500,000, or $0 (break even).

 **Spreadsheet exercise 15**

Using Goal Seek to find cost per head

1. Click on the next blank worksheet and complete the spreadsheet opposite.
2. The Total Cost of the party is dependent on the number of guests. The Cost of Food, Drink and Invites are calculated by multiplying the number of guests by the cost per head of each item. The cost of the Hall, Band and Decorations are fixed.
3. Use Goal Seek to find how many guests can be invited if the **Total Cost** is to be kept to $4000.

Skills practised:

Creating a new spreadsheet

File entering

Formula use

Goal seek function

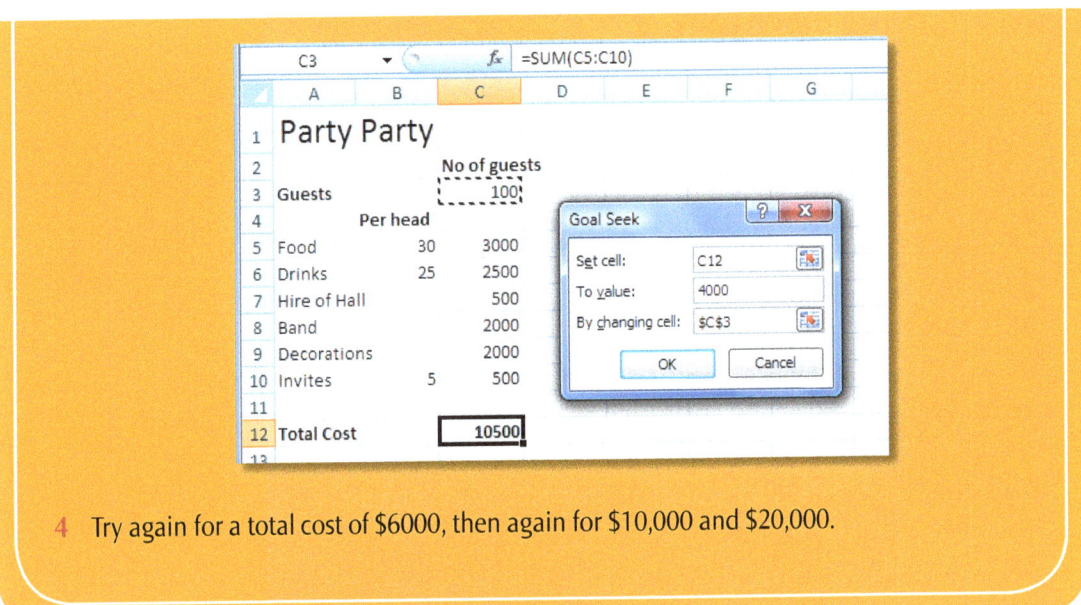

4   Try again for a total cost of $6000, then again for $10,000 and $20,000.

Spreadsheet project 1

Lawn mower extraordinaire

You are starting a lawn-mowing round to earn some extra money. You need to work out how much you will charge each customer for mowing their lawn. To work out a fee you have to determine the area of the customer's lawn. You charge 20 cents per square metre.

1   Mr Green's lawn is divided into the front lawn and back lawn. The front lawn measures 6 metres by 20 metres. The back lawn measures 15 metres by 23 metres. Create a spreadsheet that sets out:

- the customer's name
- the length and width measurements for each section of lawn
- the calculated area in square metres of each section
- the charge for each section
- a total charge to the customer.

2   Save the result for Mr Green as **Green**.

Mr Black's lawn is divided into the front lawn and back lawn. The front lawn measures 6 metres by 20 metres. The back lawn measures 15 metres by 23 metres.

3   Open the file and enter details for Mr Black, saving the file with a new name **Black**.

Mrs Plum's lawn is divided into the front lawn, side lawn and back lawn. The front lawn measures 8 metres by 24 metres. The side lawn is 4 metres by 15 metres. The back lawn measures 10 metres by 30 metres.

4   Open the Green file and enter details for Mrs Plum, saving the file with a new name **Plum**.

Challenge:

- How would you deal with lawns that had areas within them such as swimming pools and vegetables patches that you could not mow?

- How could you set up the spreadsheet so you could easily change your charge per square metre of lawn?

175

Spreadsheet project 2

1. Use your spreadsheet program to create a table that lays out your class timetable.

2. You have been collecting data on various costs associated with three different holidays. You are trying to decide which holiday to go on. Below is the data you have collected:

   - Holiday 'Surf & Ski': Lasts 10 days, the airfare is $1500, accommodation will cost $2000, living costs will be about $1000.
   - Holiday 'Red Centre': Lasts 7 days, the airfare is $2400, accommodation will cost $1800, living costs will be about $770.
   - Holiday 'Just Relax': Lasts 14 days, the airfare is $1000, accommodation will cost $3500, living costs will only be about $700 because so much is included in accommodation.

   You decide to set the data out in a spreadsheet so you can clearly see what each holiday costs in total.

   You would also like to calculate what each holiday costs per day.

MODULE 8

databases

Database terms

There are some important database terms that you will learn as you work through this topic.

Fields

Data within a database is usually divided into categories or sections called **fields**. The fields that the telephone book is divided into are:

Surname, Initials, Street Number, Street Name, Suburb, Telephone Number

These fields can vary in length, depending on how much data (characters) needs to be placed into them. For example, an Initials field does not need as much space as a Surname field. Fields can be set to different types depending on the data they need to contain. For example, fields that will contain names are set to **text fields**; fields that will contain numbers are set to **number fields**.

Records

One complete set of fields is termed a **record**. For example, each subscriber's details in the phone book is a record. There are over 1,000,000 records in the Melbourne telephone book.

Files

A complete set of records is called a **file**. The phone book is divided into two files, white pages and yellow pages. The following diagram shows the different sections of an address file.

Field Names

First name	Surname	Address	Phone number
John	Smith	25 Main Street, Belmont	52434866
Jill	Jones	101 High Street, Highton	52439022

Records

Creating a database

When you create a database the **field names** are entered followed by the **field type** that each field will contain and, for some databases, the **field width** needs to be set.

The **field type** indicates the type of data that will be entered into the field. Examples of field types include: **text**, **number**, **date** and **calculation**. The **field width** sets how many letters or numbers will be allowed in that field.

MODULE 8

databases exercise 1

Skills practised:

Adding records

Deleting records

Editing data

Saving

Printing

Creating a database

1. Create a database that allows a video store to maintain a list of its stock and save the database as **Movie Magic**.
2. Enter the following fields, field types and, if necessary, field widths.

Field name	Field type	Field width
Video Title	Text	50
Category	Text	20
Classification	Text	3
Number in Stock	Number	2
Release Year	Number	4
Price	Number	7

3. Enter the following records:

Titantic	Drama	M	5	1997	$9.95
American Beauty	Comedy	MA	1	1999	$9.95
Stuart Little	Children	G	4	2000	$12.50
StarWars II: Attack of the Clones	Fantasy	PG	5	2002	$14.95
Herbie Fully Loaded	Comedy	G	6	2004	$15.95
The Da Vinci Code	Drama	MA	4	2006	$16.95
Night at the Museum	Comedy	PG	5	2006	$16.95
License to Wed	Comedy	M	8	2007	$19.95

4. Select Save As from the Format menu, access your storage disk or folder, enter the name Movie Magic, and click on Save (or OK).
5. Print a copy of the database and check over it.

Editing a database

One of the many advantages of using a database is that changes can be made to the data at any time. New records can be added, records deleted, or the data updated in some way.

 **databases exercise 2**

Editing a database

1. Add the following records to your database from exercise 1:

| Shrek the Third | Comedy | PG | 5 | 2007 | $19.95 |
| The Simpsons Movie | Comedy | PG | 2 | 2007 | $19.95 |

2. Add some of your favourite movies to the database if you wish. Do not add more than three.
3. *American Beauty* is no longer available. Delete this record from the database.
4. The following changes need to be made:
   - the Classification of *The DaVinci Code* is M
   - the Number in Stock for *Stuart Little* is now two
   - the Release Year of *Herbie Fully Loaded* is 2005.
5. Print a list copy.

Creating reports

When information is printed from a database it is usually in the form of a **report**. Reports display the information in a concise and clear way so that the data is easy to understand. Reports can display all the data, or just sections of the data.

Reports should have:

- a **title (or main heading)**, which is usually the organisation's name
- a **sub-heading**, which is usually what the report is about
- the **current date**, so that the reader of the report can clearly see how recent the database is. It would be of little use reading a report of prices that was done 10 years ago and, because no date was provided, thinking those prices referred to today's prices.
- **page numbers**, if the report covers more than one page. Page numbers should be included at either the top or the bottom of the report.

This diagram provides an example of a database report.

```
        MAKE BELIEVE HIGH SCHOOL        ── Name of the organisation.
         YEAR 10 GEOGRAPHY MARKS        ── What the report is about.
                June, 2002              ── The date the report
                                           was prepared.

  FIRST NAME   SURNAME   TEST 1  TEST 2  TEST 3  AVERAGE
  Veronica     Callahan   34.0%   31.0%   50.0%   38.3%
  Stephen      Frederick  56.0%   72.0%   59.0%   62.3%   ── Report data under
  Janet        Hall       61.0%   58.0%   79.0%   66.0%      field headings.
  Allan        Simpson    58.0%   58.0%   42.0%   52.7%
  Dianne       Forbes     48.0%   62.0%   55.0%   55.0%
  Pauline      McAlistair 64.0%   61.0%   70.0%   65.0%


                  Page 1                  ── Page numbers required
                                             if the report covers more
                                             than one page.
```

databases exercise 3

Creating reports

Follow these steps to create a report that displays all the fields for the video database.

1. Set the title of the report to Movie Magic.
2. Set the sub-heading to Video List.
3. Insert the current date under the sub-heading and insert the page number at the bottom of the report.
4. Format the Price field to Currency with two decimal places.
5. Save the database and print a copy of the report.

Skills practised:

Creating reports

Displaying data clearly

Formatting fields

Saving

Printing

Calculation fields

Fields can do more than just store data. Fields can also do calculations such as multiplying number fields together, adding the values in fields and calculating dates.

databases exercise 4

Calculation fields

1. In your **Movie Magic** database add a new field called **Total Amount**.
2. If you are using FileMaker Pro, set the field type to calculation. If you are using Microsoft Access, create a query that contains all the fields and enter the calculation in an empty column.
3. Set the calculation to **Number In Stock*Price**. That is, multiply the number of videos in stock by their price.
4. Check that the calculation is correct for each record.
5. Resave the database.
6. Print a copy of the database.

Skills practised:

Setting calculation fields

Formatting fields

Saving

Printing

Creating different reports

One database can have numerous different reports to display a range of different information. You have just added a calculation field to your Movie Magic database, so a report to show that calculation should be provided.

databases exercise 5

Creating different reports

1. Create a new report that just lists these fields:
    - Video
    - Title
    - Release
    - Year
    - Number in stock
    - Price
    - Total amount
2. Set the title of the report to Movie Magic.
3. Set the sub-heading to Stock Inventory.
4. Include the current date just under the sub-heading.
5. Format the Price and Total amount fields to be in Currency with two decimal places.
6. Save the database and print a copy of the report.

Skills practised:

Setting calculation fields

Formatting fields

Saving

Printing

MODULE 8

Sorting data

Sorting is the process of arranging records into a particular order. You can arrange records into alphabetical, numerical or chronological (date) orders. The following diagram displays records that have been sorted into order:

Records have been sorted in LOCATION order. →

Joe's Pizza Palaces
Employee Details
10/4.00

First Name	Surname	Birth date	Position	Location	Hours	Payrate
Rita	Bertoli	6/5/72	Manager	Essendon	40	$18.00
Tony	Bertoli	4/8/75	Cook	Essendon	36	$15.00
Kevin	Browne	14/12/77	Cook	Essendon	35	$15.00
Anthony	Hall	29/4/70	Delivery	Essendon	35	$11.00
Stuart	Thompson	5/3/79	Waiter	Essendon	25	$12.50
David	Barrett	2/4/70	Manager	Keilor	40	$18.00
Andrew	Conrads	12/180	Cook	Keilor	38	$15.00
Mario	Costa	17/9/75	Waiter	Keilor	35	$12.50
Gail	Norris	10/12/81	Delivery	Keilor	30	$11.00
Robert	Stojanovski	13/3/78	Delivery	Keilor	35	$11.00
Maree	Tizard	18/11/65	Cook	Keilor	25	$15.00

 **databases** exercise 6

Sorting data

1. Sort the Movie Magic database into video title order. This should arrange the records so that the video titles are in alphabetical order. Print a copy of your first report created in exercise 3.

2. Sort the database into number in stock order, with the most in stock listed first down to the least. This should arrange the records so that the stock numbers are listed in descending order. Print a copy of your second report created in exercise 5.

3. Sort the database into release year then video title order. This should arrange the records so they are in release date order. If any of the videos are released in the same year they should be listed in alphabetical order. Print a copy of your first report.

Skills practised:

Sorting alphabetically

Sorting numerically

Sorting chronologically

Saving

Printing

Finding data

Databases allow you to display just part of the data. Some databases call this process searching, others call it querying. For example, a school might wish to just display details for the girls, or all the students who travel to school by bus, or those students who speak a language other than English.

databases exercise 7

Finding data

1. In your Movie Magic database, find all the videos whose category is set to Drama. Print a copy of your first report from exercise 3.
2. Find all the videos that were released in 2007 and print a copy of your second report from exercise 5.
3. Find all the videos that have five copies in stock. Sort the records into video title order and print a copy of your first report.
4. Find all the videos whose total amount is greater than $70. Sort the records into total amount order (descending) and print a copy of your second report.
5. Find all the videos that have fewer than five copies in stock. Sort the records into total amount order (descending) and print a copy of your second report.

Skills practised:

Setting fields

Entering data

Formatting data

Finding data

Sorting data

Reporting

Saving

Printing

databases exercise 8

Creating another database

To practise what you have learnt in these exercises, create another database. This time, record borrowing details for members of the Movie Magic Video Store. Members are allowed to borrow videos for two nights.

1. Create a new database with the following fields:

Field Name	Field Type	Field Width
First Name	Text	15
Surname	Text	15
Video	Text	50
Date Borrowed	Date	10

2. Add a Calculation field called Date Due, which adds two days to the Date Borrowed field. That is: = Date Borrowed + 2

3 Enter the following records:

Julie	Harrison	Titanic	12/2/2010
Mark	Colletta	Herbie Fully Loaded	13/2/2010
Maria	Sarcevic	The Da Vinci Code	13/2/2010
Paul	O'Brien	Titanic	14/2/2010
Andrea	Hall	Stuart Little	14/2/2010
Barry	Robinson	Herbie Fully Loaded	14/2/2010
Katie	Jamison	Licensed To Wed	14/2/2010
Graeme	McKenzie	Herbie Fully Loaded	15/2/2010

4 Save the database as **Video Borrowing**.
5 Create a report that lists all the fields with the title report set to **Movie Magic**, the sub-heading set to **Borrowings for February 2010** and insert the current date under the sub-heading.
6 Sort the data into **Date Due** then **Surname** order. Print a copy of the report.
7 Delete Julie Harrison's record, as she has returned the video.
8 Find all the videos due on 14/2/2010, as these are overdue. Print a copy of the report.
9 Find who has borrowed *Herbie Fully Loaded* and print another copy of the report.

Databases project

Old actors database

Your grandfather is a lover of old movies. You can't see the attraction, but you have decided for his birthday to create a database of trivia about old actors for him.

The database will require the following fields: First Name, Last Name, Real Name, Year Born, Country and Number of Academy Awards. The data is displayed on the opposite page.

When the data has been entered, two reports are needed:

1 A column report displaying all the data. For this report print:
   a all the records sorted in alphabetical order by Last Name
   b just the actors born in the USA
   c just the actors born before 1920.
2 A column report showing First Name, Last Name Real Name and Academy Awards. For this report print just the Academy Award winners.

Investigate the problem

Plan the field types that will be required and the different types of reports that will be needed. Draw a field list table, referring to the one in exercise 1.

Design the solution

Draw thumbnail sketches of the different reports that you will create. Include the headings and sub-headings that will be required, the fonts and sizes that you intend to use, the width of the columns or fields, how the report will be sorted and what searches will be required, etc.

Produce the solution

Enter the fields and then enter the data shown below. Create the necessary reports, sort them into the required order, carry out the required searches and print copies of the reports.

Evaluate the solution

1. How many actors have won an Academy Award?
2. Which actor has won the most Academy Awards?
3. What extra fields do you think your grandfather might want to add to the database?
4. What will be the advantages to your grandfather of having this data in a database?

Old Actors Data

John	Wayne	Marion Morrison	1907	USA	1
Marilyn	Monroe	Norma Jean Baker	1926	USA	–
Cary	Grant	Archibald Leach	1904	UK	–
Rock	Hudson	Roy Scherer	1925	USA	–
Judy	Garland	Frances Gumm	1922	USA	2
Boris	Karloff	William Pratt	1887	UK	–
Doris	Day	Doris Von Kappelhoff	1924	USA	–
Mickey	Rooney	Joe Yule Jr.	1920	USA	1
Charles	Bronson	Charles Buchinsky	1921	USA	–
Lauren	Becall	Betty Perske	1924	USA	1
Kirk	Douglas	Issar Danielowitch	1916	USA	–

Index

A
access, 13
action buttons, 125
aligning objects, 92
aligning text, 57
animated movies, 3
animating Clip Art, 116
animating slides, 116
antivirus software, 19
ARANET, 23
ATM, 9, 12
attachments, 42
Australian Academics Research Network (AARNET), 24

B
back-up data, 17, 18
back-ups, 21
banking, 3, 23
bit-map programs, 135
bits, 15
bold, 52
bookmarks, 38
broadband, 26–7
browser, 27, 31
bulleted lists, 62
bulletin boards, 28
bytes, 15

C
calculation fields, 182
calculations, 157, 159–64
cash registers, 9, 12
CD drive, 14, 17
charts, 167–71
chat rooms, 45, 46
Clip Art, 10, 87-9, 112–13
combining photos, 147
communication, 3, 11, 23
computer crime, 20
computer games, 3
computer graphics, 134
computer theft, 20
computers (development of), 4
copying graphics, 139
copying text, 54
Corel Draw, 12
credibility, 36
custom action buttons, 127
customised programs, 12
cutting text, 54

D
data (input of) 6, 12
data entry, 159
database editing, 181
database terms, 174
dial-up, 27
digital camera, 7, 10, 11
disk drive, 7
domain name, 28
DOS, 13
drawing programs, 135
drawing shapes, 81
DVD drive, 14
DVDs, 8

E
Edit Marquee, 139
editing graphics, 140
editing photos, 141
education, 3, 24–5
email attachments, 42
email, 3, 4, 23, 28, 39–42
etiquette, 39, 41
Excel, 13

F
Facebook, 43
favourites, 38
fields, 179
file transfer protocol (FTP), 27
files, 11, 15–17, 179
filling shapes, 84
finding data, 185
firewalls, 19, 21
flash drive, 14
floppy disk drive, 7
folders, 15–17
fonts, 52
footers, 66
format menu, 52, 57
formatting bullets, 62
formatting, 52
formulas, 159–61
fraud, 20, 26

G
games, 12
Goal Seek, 172–5
Google, 29–30
governments, 24
graphical user interface, 12–13
graphics programs, 135
graphics, 67–8

H

hackers, 20
hanging indent, 60, 68
hard disk, 14, 15
hard drive, 14
hardware, 6, 10
headers, 66–8
health and safety, 42–5
hyperlinks, 32, 33, 128
hypertext transfer protocol (http), 27

I

inbox, 41
indent, 58, 60–1, 64
information technology, 3
inserting movie files, 124
interactive learning, 25
interface, 12–13
internet (disadvantages of), 26
internet relay chat (IRL), 27–8
internet safety, 42–6
internet service provider (ISP), 26–7
internet, 3, 23–6
IT, 3
italics, 52

K

keyboard technique, 49
keyboards, 7, 10, 49

L

leader characters, 63
Linux, 13
local area network (LAN) 23, 24

M

Macintosh Desktop, 16
Macintosh, 13
mailing lists, 28
margins, 58
masks, 149
memory, 6, 14
Microsoft Word, 12–13
millennium bug, 12
mobile phone, 9
modem, 7, 11, 26
monitor, 7
mouse, 7, 32
movie clips, 124
movie files, 97
   importing files, 97–8
   motion and video effects, 99–100
   adding titles, 100
   sound tracks, 102
   editing movies, 103–4
   exporting movies, 104
   preparing DVDs, 105
movies, 3
moving text, 55
MP3 player, 7
multimedia, 109
multiple-page documents, 68
music, 3

N

Netalert, 45, 46
netiquette, 35
networks, 11, 14, 21, 23
newsgroups, 28
newsletters, 72–3

O

objects, 82–3
online education, 24
operating systems, 12–13
output devices, 7, 8, 10, 14

P

page breaks, 55
page margins, 58–9
Paint programs, 135
painting, 135–6
passwords, 18
pasting text, 54
peripheral devices, 8, 11
peripherals, 7
photo editing, 141
Photoshop, 135
pixel-based programs, 135
posture, 50
Powerpoint, 13, 109
presentations, 109–15
print preview, 53
printer 7, 11
programs, 7, 11–12
protocols, 23

R

random-access memory (RAM), 14
read-only memory (ROM), 14
records, 179
reports, 181–3

S

safety, 42–5
scanner, 7, 10, 12
screen, 7
search engine, 30, 33–5

sections, 69–70
security, 17, 21, 44–5
servers, 39
shadow effects, 85
shape fills, 84
shape outline, 85
shapes, 81
sketching, 137
Slide Master, 118
slide transitions, 115
SmartArt Graphics, 91–2
software, 12
sorting data, 184
speakers, 7
special effects, 146
spreadsheets, 13, 157
standard programs, 12
storage, 14, 15
subfolders, 15
system unit, 7

T

tab stops, 57, 63
tabs, 60–1, 64
technology (development of), 10
Text Box tool, 86–7
toolbar, 52
touch screen, 7

U

underline, 52
universal resource locator (URL), 27
UNIX, 13
using WordArt, 89–90

V

vector-based programs, 135
video files, 97
video, 8
viruses, 19–20, 26
voice recognition, 10

W

wide-area network (WAN) 23, 24
Windows Explorer, 16
Windows, 12–13, 15
wireless technology, 11, 26–7
word processing, 12, 49, 74–5
word wrap, 50
world wide web (www), 27

Y

Y2K, 12

For EU product safety concerns, contact us at Calle de José Abascal, 56–1°,
28003 Madrid, Spain or eugpsr@cambridge.org.

www.ingramcontent.com/pod-product-compliance
Ingram Content Group UK Ltd.
Pitfield, Milton Keynes, MK11 3LW, UK
UKHW051239180426
11947UKWH00013B/865